The Philadelphia Anthropological Society

PAPERS PRESENTED
ON ITS
GOLDEN ANNIVERSARY

The Philadelphia

Anthropological Society

PAPERS PRESENTED
ON ITS
GOLDEN ANNIVERSARY

Edited by Jacob W. Gruber

1967

Temple University Publications

DISTRIBUTED BY

COLUMBIA UNIVERSITY PRESS

NEW YORK & LONDON

Jacob W. Gruber is Professor of Anthropology at Temple University in Philadelphia. He edited these papers, which were read in a day-long session at the fiftieth anniversary of the Philadelphia Anthropological Society held at the University of Pennsylvania Museum on October 12, 1962. He is the author of *A Conscience in Conflict: The Life of St. George Jackson Mivart.*

Preface

IT IS commonplace in anthropology to invest ceremony with social function. Anniversaries of one sort or another not only serve to reestablish the conditions of the initial event, but also provide the opportunity to review history. By making apparent the landmarks of "then" and "now" the anniversary permits a retrospect, a tentative summing up, which serves also as a stimulus for the future.

As Professor Hallowell notes in this volume, the Philadelphia Anthropological Society was born from the need of anthropologists to communicate with one another; and from meeting to meeting and from year to year, its existence and its form followed this need. Its members were not particularly interested in its history or in the intricacies of its organizational structure; its records, except those which exist in memory, are fragmentary at best. It was, as it is, a heuristic device for the stimulation of communication among anthropologists.

Anthropologists, however, are not so alien to the society in which they exist that they cannot be affected by the recollection theme of our own culture which gives rise to centenaries, bicentenaries, semi-centenaries—birthdays of every description and variety. Thus, even though the real date was unknown, as the general period of the fiftieth anniversary of the beginnings of the Philadelphia Anthropological Society approached, there was the call for some means to celebrate the occasion. The call was translated into action by the President, William B. Schwab, through the appointment of a committee to plan an appropriate program to honor the Society on its fiftieth birthday. The committee consisted of A. I. Hallowell as chairman and Frederica de Laguna, Jacob W. Gruber, and J. Alden Mason, a group which represented not only the local institutions providing anthropological instruction, but also the continuity of membership of the Society.

When the members of the program committee first met, they

came to one immediate and unanimous decision: It was thought that this celebration provided the opportunity for assembling a series of papers by invited speakers which might be devoted to selected aspects of American anthropology considered in historical perspective; and, because of the local nature of the Society, it was also felt that it would be interesting and instructive to suggest the role which Philadelphia itself played as a center of anthropological interest and activity. Anthropologists without portfolio were to be found here long before anthropology became an academic discipline or a professional enterprise; and the city has, at various times, pioneered in both anthropological instruction and research. The invited papers as they were read during a day-long session on October 12, 1962, and as they appear in this volume, reflect that "pride of place" which directed the planning of the committee.

The nature of anthropology as a discipline and its own recency led to some feelings of self-consciousness on the part of the committee, as the historical view must lead to feelings of uneasiness with most of the practicing anthropologists. Developments in anthropology are recent; and despite the nineteenth-century origins of the field, anthropology, as most of its practitioners know it, is essentially a twentieth-century product, whose pioneers have been known personally to most of the present generation. We are, in a sense, in the presence of our elders and it seems pretentious to translate them to the venerable status of culture hero. As David Goddard, Provost of the University of Pennsylvania and the son of a distinguished American anthropologist, noted in his welcome:

It is interesting to think what anthropology must have been like fifty years ago. At that point it was a new academic science, and Franz Boas was at the height of his powers at Columbia University. The department at Berkeley consisted of Alfred Kroeber and T. T. Waterman. At the American Museum the department was small, with Clark Wissler, Pliny E. Goddard, and Nels Nelson, recently transferred from Berkeley. Roland Dixon started anthropological teaching at Harvard, and Frank Speck, George Gordon and Wilson Wallis were teaching at Pennsylvania.

It is interesting to realize that within a lifetime one can have known the founders of American anthropology and yet greet the active workers in the field today. I had the good fortune to grow up in an anthropologist's home. I first met Alden Mason and Frank Speck when they came to spend the night at my father's house in New Jersey. I used to drive

Franz Boas into the country, as he did not himself drive a car. I was particularly fortunate in having had two courses in anthropology from Alfred Kroeber, the first to take a Ph.D. under Boas at Columbia University, and a man who was with us with vigor and insight until two years ago. I also had one course with Robert Lowie.

The continuity and the recency of history are even more apparent when we look back and see vaguely and mistily what anthropology was about and what anthropologists were doing fifty years ago at the time of the first anthropological meeting of the Philadelphia Anthropological Society. If one leafs through the pages of the *American Anthropologist* or if one reads the reviews in the then newly established and soon deceased *Current Anthropological Literature*, one notices how similar in approach, in arguments, in point of view, and in breadth of coverage the anthropology of 1912 was to the anthropology of today. As one reads the articles, he is aware how little change there has been in the dimension of the field and how close the past is to the present. The great names of American anthropology, those who formed its heroic age, are there: Hrdlička, Lowie, Fewkes, Wissler, Tozzer, Dixon, Alice Fletcher, Sapir, Swanton, Kidder, Wallis, Chamberlain, Kroeber, and, of course, Boas. The watershed between the anthropology of the nineteenth century and that of the twentieth century is emphasized by the obituaries of Andrew Lang, Topinard, and Keane, all of whom in the post-Darwinian period had actively sought to build a science of man and whose writings provided that science with much of its excitement, novelty, and popular interest.

Here, interestingly enough, is a review of Jane Harrison's *Themis* by Hooton. Here is Lowie's attack on the psychic unity of mankind as well as his discussion, initiated in *Science*, of the differences between the American and British schools of anthropology. Here are the papers of a symposium on culture and environment, including papers by Sapir and Wissler; and here is Swanton's work on the social organization of the Creek and Goldenweiser's "The Origins of Totemism." By their subject matter none of these papers would be out of place in a current issue of the *Anthropologist;* each represents the continuity, the centrality of anthropology as a self-contained and self-conscious discipline.

In noting the continuity over the past half century, it is instructive and perhaps humbling to see something of the nature of the field itself a half-century ago as a focus of professional involvement. It had been only ten years earlier that the American Anthropological Association had itself been organized at the meetings of the American Association for the Advancement of Science in Pittsburgh; and a year later the affiliation of the newly formed Association and the American Folklore Society with Section H of the AAAS—long the clearing house for anthropological studies in the United States—led George Grant MacCurdy to announce "the unification of all anthropological interests strictly national in scope."

Boas' *Kwakiutl Tales* had only recently initiated Columbia University's Contributions to Anthropology, a development which, along with a series initiated earlier by Harvard, Pennsylvania, and California, led Sapir to note that "it is decidedly encouraging to find the universities sharing in the growth of anthropological interest in America, not merely by providing for academic courses in the subject, but also by publishing the results of anthropological research." Despite the professionalization which the new organization conferred upon its members and upon the discipline, and despite the breadth and extent of the anthropological activities pursued, professional academic training and preparation were still scant. In the United States the first doctorate in anthropology was conferred upon Alexander Chamberlain in 1892, and by 1912 only about twenty degrees had been granted from six institutions. Anthropologists were based primarily in museums; and their activities were augmented by a number of reports from others whose non-anthropological professional activities provided them with the opportunities to collect data of anthropological interest. Questions of methodology and problems of analysis were becoming increasingly important as the necessary breakthroughs had occurred in the collection of data; and it was inevitable that the increasing emphasis upon methodology and an increasing refinement of anthropological problems should lead to more sophisticated concepts of field work through which alone the necessary data for anthropology could be accumulated.

There was still, fifty years ago, a great deal of "amateur" involvement in anthropology, so characteristic of science generally during the nineteenth century. In contrast to other disciplines, anthropology's involvement of the nonprofessional, radically reduced in some areas, has never ceased, a feature which provided the subject—

notably archaeology—with something of its definition and its popular virtue as a scientific discipline.

The papers that follow constitute the proceedings of the anniversary meeting. They are not designed to create any sense of nostalgia for the past or to revive for our own amusement the quaintness of our intellectual ancestors. They are, in effect, summaries of what has been done in Philadelphia by Philadelphians to create the present structure of anthropology. The coverage is unbalanced as Philadelphia's contributions to anthropology were unbalanced. Because of the stimulus inherent in the existence of the University Museum, there has been a necessary emphasis upon archaeology—and, particularly, New World archaeology; and one cannot ignore the fact that the presence of Frank G. Speck as an integral part of Philadelphia anthropology led to some emphasis upon the peoples and cultures of the Northeast Woodlands. These papers, therefore, should not be read, as they were not intended to be, as an inventory of the present state of American anthropology. They are contributions to a history of anthropology which, in the main, describe the role of Philadelphia and the Philadelphia Anthropological Society in the emergence and development of anthropology. As documents of this sort they are timeless; and their timelessness may excuse the long delay in their appearance.

It is necessary, finally, to express appreciation to Dr. A. I. Hallowell who, as chairman of the anniversary committee, had manifested a continuing interest in the publication of this volume, and to Miss Barbara Bloomfield, who undertook the editorial revisions in the manuscripts which were necessary to make them ready for publication.

It is also proper here to acknowledge with gratitude the financial aid provided by the University of Pennsylvania, University Museum, Temple University, Bryn Mawr College, and the Wenner-Gren Foundation, which made it possible to assemble the participants in this meeting. And, of course, neither the meeting itself nor this volume could have come about without the cooperation and patience of the authors themselves.

J. W. G.

Temple University
July 1967

Contents

The Philadelphia Anthropological Society

PAPERS PRESENTED
ON ITS
GOLDEN ANNIVERSARY

A. IRVING HALLOWELL

Anthropology in Philadelphia

THE Philadelphia Anthropological Society has been unique, perhaps, insofar as it has never been exclusively an organization of
professional anthropologists. Nor has it had any formal affiliations
with educational institutions in this area (although it has never
spurned their facilities). The Society has remained independent,
highly flexible and fluctuating in personnel, while at the same time it
has constantly reflected in microcosm what has been currently happening in anthropology at large. What it has done all along is to
provide an open forum for the serious discussion of all phases of
anthropology for those interested in attending its meetings. It has
never attempted to popularize its lectures, or to attract the general
public.

The Society did not start with a bang. It had a humble beginning
and it remained small in numbers for many years. Documents for
the earliest period are sadly lacking, so that we do not know all we
should like to know about those years. We do know that prior to
World War I a few men interested in anthropological problems
met, more or less regularly, with Frank G. Speck in a downtown
restaurant (some have called it a saloon!) for dinner. So we must
honor Speck as our founder (J. A. Mason, 1950a).[1] Fortunately we
have a list of speakers from 1914 on. In that year, William Chur-

[1] Referring to Speck as the founder of the Society, Mason goes on to say:
"Probably no one now remembers, or ever remembered, when it actually
began, for it commenced with an informal group meeting for dinner at
Ostendorffs', a Philadelphia restaurant that has long since disappeared, where
Frank could indulge his liking for oyster stew." Mrs. Speck tells me that the
group sometimes met at their home. The year selected for the celebration of
the anniversary was determined by Speck's recollection of the year when the
dinners at Ostendorffs' began. Speck served in the more formal capacity of
President of the Society from 1920 to 1922. (See J. A. Mason, 1950c, where
some of these facts are more briefly stated.)

chill, well known at the time as a student of Polynesian linguistics and ethnology, is listed; and for 1915 we find the name of Ralph Linton, who took his master's degree at the University of Pennsylvania.

By the time I attended my first meeting in 1916, the established meeting place had been shifted to the University campus. I made my way upstairs to a small room on the third floor of Houston Hall. I was almost overwhelmed by the aura of dignity I encountered. There were scarcely a dozen people present. They were all men of scholarly mien. When I tiptoed to a seat they were quietly awaiting the arrival of the speaker. The latter, when he appeared, wore a beard and was tightly buttoned up in a long frock coat. He was a great scholar—W. Max Müller, the Egyptologist. His topic was "Experiences of a Linguist in North Africa." This is the first and last time I have ever seen a frock coat at any sort of anthropological meeting. Beards have sprouted again, but I fancy frock coats have disappeared forever.

There were no women present at this meeting because their presence was taboo. In fact, there was a hot debate soon afterwards before the rules were finally changed and women could become members. It was only then that Miss H. Newell Wardle, a founder of the American Anthropological Association, and at that time connected with the Academy of Natural Sciences, could be invited to join the Philadelphia Anthropological Society. There was certainly a cultural lag here, but the pattern was a repetition of events that had previously occurred in anthropological circles. In Washington, in the eighties of the last century, a group of women under the leadership of Alice Fletcher organized the Women's Anthropological Society of Washington, presumably as a reaction to exclusion from male discussion in that city (Lurie, 1966).[2] These women must have been terribly serious-minded and self-conscious, because they even banned refreshments on principle. An Anthropolocial Society meeting was not to be confused with a pink tea! However,

[2] Among the exhibits prepared by the Smithsonian Institution, when the annual meetings of the American Anthropological Association were held in Washington (1958) was one devoted to the Woman's Anthropological Society of Washington. This organization, founded in 1885, included civic activities which may be viewed as an early example of applied anthropology.

this group merged with the Anthropological Society of Washington in 1899, when 49 women were elected members of the men's organization at one fell swoop. Perhaps it was highly symbolic when, in Philadelphia, our first woman speaker (1920) was Elsie Clews Parsons. Her thesis in *The Old Fashioned Woman* (1913), it may be recalled, was to show, on the basis of comparative ethnographic data, how women in our society were thwarted by archaic attitudes. On the occasion of this meeting we had to move to College Hall because no women were allowed above the first floor of Houston Hall at night.

At a later period we held dinner meetings in the old Lido Restaurant on Woodland Avenue. It was here, I believe, that Lévy-Bruhl was our speaker, one of a series of foreign scholars who addressed us. These include Sir Peter Buck, J. H. Driberg, Daryll Forde, Julius Lips, C. G. Seligmann, D. H. Westermann, Sir Solly Zuckerman, and others. As for American colleagues, so many have spoken to us that I shall mention none. If I did so it would be a roll call of most of the distinguished anthropologists in the United States during the past generation. I will only say that we never have been able to pay honoraria. Yet we seem to have been eminently successful in prevailing upon the good will of our friends over many years.

Perhaps I should add that we have likewise had a number of speakers from fields other than anthropology. From psychology, for example, I recall W. Köhler and Ray Carpenter. The latter talked to us and showed us his movies long before most anthropologists had shown any interest in infrahuman primate behavior. Our presidents, too, have sometimes been drawn from other disciplines. Our oldest living past president, W. W. Hyde, is Professor Emeritus of Classics and Ancient History, now in his ninth decade of life.[3] J. W. Harshberger, Professor of Botany at the time and chairman of the department, was the author of a pioneer monograph, *Maize*, published in 1893. From Sumerology we have had Samuel Kramer; from business, Percy C. Madeira, Jr.; and from sociology, my old friend, the late James W. Woodard of Temple University.

Without deliberation, or set policy, the Philadelphia Anthropological Society throughout its history appears to have embraced the

[3] Professor Hyde is recently deceased.

inclusive conception of anthropology—in membership, officers, and speakers—which has characterized American anthropology as a whole. During the period 1914 to 1937, we heard about European archaeology and American archaeology; we listened to Orientalists and some Africanists; we heard cross-cousin marriage discussed and the devil worshippers of Kurdistan described; we were told about the pygmies of Dutch New Guinea and we were given accounts of Tungus and of African folk tales; we learned about racial studies in Polynesia and the heredity of body build. In 1921 Waterman gave us an account of the discovery of Ishi,[4] and in 1932 we had a talk on "Personality and Primitive Culture" by Kroeber.

I ask you now to follow me back into the more distant past, in order that the Philadelphia Anthropological Society may be seen in wider historical perspective as one of the many activities of anthropological interest that have had Philadelphia as their locale. But, just as we have no fully rounded account of the earliest years of our Society, because no one took the trouble to collect the information, in the same way, on a longer historical scale, we have no fully rounded account of what now would be recognized as matters of anthropological interest in the history of Philadelphia. References have been made today to fragments of this story, particularly to the role of members of the American Philosophical Society at a very early date. Here I wish to recall some facts which have aroused my personal interest, as I hope they may arouse yours.

Recently I ran across a reference to an Eskimo collection, presented to the venerable Library Company of Philadelphia in 1754. Was this the first ethnological collection exhibited here? And why did it turn up in Philadelphia? The answer is relatively simple if it is recalled that Philadelphians in the eighteenth century combined all sorts of intellectual interests with a spirit of enterprise. In 1753 a number of Philadelphia gentlemen, including Benjamin Franklin, fitted out a vessel to be sent in search of the Northwest Passage as well as possible lucrative trade on the coast of Labrador. The ship never accomplished its geographical aims, nor did it bring back the

[4] The full story of Ishi has now been beautifully expounded and fully documented by Theodora Kroeber (1961).

Golden Fleece, but it did reach Davis Strait. A collection of Eskimo garments and artifacts was made, which, "when presented to the Library as a gift from the 'North-West Company,' became one of the most popular exhibits in its growing museum." [5]

This example is indicative of the historical circumstances under which exotic objects from distant parts of the world originally were brought to the attention of the public in urban centers in the days before professional anthropologists existed. Another way in which such material was assembled and sometimes carefully studied was through the activities of private collectors. Pierre Eugene Du Simitière (1736–1784) was one such man in Philadelphia who perhaps deserves more attention than he has received. He was a miniature painter and a passionate collector of everything from documents to natural history. He opened his collection to public gaze on Arch Street in 1782. Among other things he was interested in Indian "antiquities." But he did more than collect and exhibit. If you will consult the notebooks he left, you will find the kind of exact descriptions of objects and their provenience which foreshadow a part of our anthropological tradition. He records, for example, that stone hatchets of various sizes and forms came from a certain field in New Jersey a little west of Trenton Ferry; that a "maneto-face mask of an Indian conjurer," has a "border of bear skin round the forehead and a tuft of feathers in the center," and that it was sent to him by George Clinton. Du Simitière, moreover, appears to have sensed that he was pioneering, since in 1770, apropos of his "Indian Antiquities" he says: ". . . it is a new subject and not touched upon by authors" (Potts, 1889, p. 349; Huth, 1945; Levey, 1951; Pennsyl-

---

[5] "In the thirties the efforts of Benjamin Franklin and the patronage of James Logan had assisted a group of Philadelphia tradesmen and a few gentlemen associates to the formation of the Library company, upon which the Proprietors conferred a plot of land and a charter in 1742. The acquisitions of this organization during its first two decades of existence reflect the primary desire of its middle-class members for serious books and volumes of instruction on a variety of subjects" (Bridenbaugh, 1942, p. 86). At the same time the Library Company paralleled "its collections of Books with a cabinet containing scientific apparatus and natural curiosities, to which the Eskimo collection . . . constituted a considerable addition." A cabinet of fossils was also accumulated, and a collection of medals considered to be of great value in the study of Roman history (*ibid.*, p. 353).

vania Historical Records Survey, 1940).[6] The date is long prior to the meeting of the American Philosophical Society in 1797, over which Thomas Jefferson presided and at which "a plan for collecting information respecting the antiquities of North America" was first considered.[7]

Charles Willson Peale (1741–1827) was another painter-collector. In his younger days he had mastered the saddler's trade, taught himself painting, fought in the Revolution, and served briefly in the Pennsylvania Assembly. Later he became a member of the American Philosophical Society. He was renowned for his portraits of eminent contemporaries. Meriwether Lewis and William Clark, the leaders of the most famous exploratory expedition in American history, were among those who sat for him.[8] The new knowledge acquired by their expedition—geographical, mineralogical, botanical, zoological—included information on the native Indian population of the vast unknown country west of the Mississippi. It first became available in print in Biddle's *History* (1814), which De Voto characterizes as "the first reliable account of whatever length, of the Western tribes." He goes on to say: "It put a valuable bulk of knowledge at the disposal of anyone who had interest in or use for knowledge relating to the Indians of the West. So it has always been a prime source for anthropologists and historians" (De Voto, 1953, p. lii). Inquiry along ethnological lines was explicitly incorporated and set forth in Jefferson's overall instructions to Lewis (Jackson,

[6] Bridenbaugh (1942, p. 354) says: "a most careful and systematically projected scheme for an 'American Museum' was evolved by the humble miniature painter, antiquary and naturalist Pierre Du Simitière, who had devoted his entire life to the assembling of materials and specimens for a natural and civil history of America. . . . Without benefit of great wealth, the persistent curiosity of this Swiss craftsman brought together much the same sort of collection as that which Sir Hans Sloane made the foundation of the British Museum. It was most unfortunate that at the time of his death in 1784 the General Assembly of Pennsylvania considered it 'not expedient or consistent with the state of the treasury' for the state to purchase and preserve his collections, refusal of which had been granted it by his will."

[7] Reference is to the Standing Committee on Antiquities of the American Philosophical Society noted by Freeman in this volume. For further information see Chinard (1943).

[8] These portraits, in the collections of Independence National Historical Park in downtown Philadelphia, are photographically reproduced in Jackson (1962).

1962, No. 47, p. 62).[9] Besides this, a list of more than one hundred specific topics was drawn up, which provided a comprehensive outline to be followed in the collection of demographic facts and ethnographic data. Several eminent Philadelphians, personally known to Jefferson as fellow members of the American Philosophical Society, were confidentially informed about the expedition in its earliest planning stage. Since it was impractical to send specialists on the expedition, Lewis was sent to consult with them as men learned beyond the boundary of their own specialty. It was these men who were specifically asked to contribute to the topical questionnaire on the Indians with which the explorers were later provided. Dr. Benjamin Rush (1745?–1813), who had long before (1774) published his pioneer *Enquiry into the Natural History of Medicine Among the Indians in North-America and a Comparative View of their Diseases and Remedies with those of Civilized Nations,* was an important contributor,[10] Dr. Caspar Wistar (1761–1818) [11] and Dr. Benjamin Smith Barton (1766–1815), probably less so.[12] This ques-

[9] For categorical reference to the kind of information to be sought on the Indian population, see Jackson (1962, p. 62).

[10] Jefferson solicited the aid of Rush, a professor of medicine at the University of Pennsylvania and a leading American physician, in February 1803 (see Jackson, 1962, No. 13). In addition to contributing some suggested inquiries "relative to the natural history of the Indians," the questions were arranged under three headings: Physical History and Medicine, Morals, and Religion. Under Morals, in addition to other questions, we find: "Is Suicide common among them?—ever from love?" Under Religion he asked: "How do they dispose of their dead, and with what ceremonies do they inter them?" Rush already had devoted some thought to these matters, since he had given some questions to Alexander McGillivray (Chief of the Creeks) in 1790, and to Timothy Pickering in 1791 when the latter visited the Seneca (*ibid.,* p. 51n). See also pp. 157–60 and note for Clark's more elaborate list of questions (1804), based on Rush, with possible additions from Wistar and Barton.

[11] The questions suggested by Wistar have not survived, but the material may have been incorporated in Clark's later list (Jackson, 1962, No. 71 and note). Jefferson wrote to Wistar in much the same vein as he had written to Rush (*ibid.,* No. 12).

[12] Barton was a physician who was a lecturer at the University of Pennsylvania and who was interested in natural history as well as Indian ethnography and linguistics. For information on his linguistic work see Greene (1960). Jefferson's confidential letter to Barton in February 1803 (Jackson, 1962, No. 11) informs him about the proposed expedition under the leadership of Lewis and then goes on to say: "In order to draw his attention at once to the objects most desirable, I must ask the favor of you to prepare for him a note on the

tionnaire approach, initiated by Jefferson, set a precedent followed for a long time thereafter in the collection of data on the American aborigines.

Peale's interest in the collection and exhibition of objects in the field of natural history (including Indian "relics") culminated in his American Museum, the first natural history museum in America.[13] Begun in 1784 and at first quartered in an extension which Peale added to his home on Lombard Street, it gained national status a decade later when it was moved, or more literally paraded, into the new building the Philosophical Society had erected near Independence Hall. Here, in the early years of the nineteenth century, in addition to being able to see the famous mounted skeleton of a mastodon, more than a thousand stuffed birds, specimens of minerals, and a large number of portraits painted by Peale and his three sons, visitors were uniquely privileged to see a collection of objects from Indian tribes of the far West collected by Lewis and Clark. For Lewis shipped specimens of all kinds to Jefferson—minerals,

---

lines of botany, zoology, or of Indian history which you think most worthy of inquiry and observation. He will be with you in Philadelphia in two or three weeks, and will wait on you, and receive thankfully on paper, and any verbal communication which you may be so good as to make him." In a letter to Jefferson sent from Philadelphia in May, Lewis says that he has seen all three men mentioned above. He notes that Rush already had submitted queries and that "Drs. Barton and Wistar have each promised to contribute in like manner anything which may suggest itself to them as being of any importance in furthering the objects of this expedition" (*ibid.*, No. 40). Later Barton prepared inquiries on the customs and languages of the Indians for the expedition of Thomas Nuttall in 1810–1811, but Jackson (p. 161n) is doubtful whether Barton actually contributed any questions to Lewis and Clark. When Thwaites published his edition of the *Journals* of the expedition in 1904–1905, he included in the appendix to Vol. 7 (1904, pp. 283–87), a section titled, "Ethnological Information Desired." This was the first time that the detailed questionnaire prepared for use on the expedition had been printed in full. Although the manuscript which survives is in the handwriting of Clark, the editor of these volumes considered it to be a "transcript of instructions from Jefferson" (Hallowell, 1960, p. 17n; for additional information on the Lewis and Clark expedition in anthropological perspective see pp. 37–38). Consult the same essay for the later use of the notes and queries approach by Lewis Cass and the Smithsonian Institution.

13 See Simpson (1942, p. 262) who says it was "probably the first of American public natural history museums, to be definitely founded and organized as such."

animal skins, plants, seeds, and examples of Indian handicrafts, weapons, and utensils—and most of these were passed on to Peale for exhibition in his museum.[14] A contemporary observer in the 1820s says that on entering the "Long Room," there could be seen in a corner case "a wax figure of Col. Lewis or Clark, I do not remember which, in a complete Indian costume. The case of the Indians and their dresses and implements were very attractive" (Colton, 1909, p. 230).

The figure referred to undoubtedly was Lewis. In a letter which Peale wrote to Jefferson in January 1808, he says: "A few weeks past I completed a wax figure of Captn. Lewis and placed it in the Museum, my object in this work is to give a lesson to the Indians who may visit the Museum, and also to shew my sentiments respecting wars. The Figure being dressed in an Indian Dress presented to Captn. Lewis by *Comeahwait*, Chief of the Shoshone Nation [and brother of Sacagawea], who was suspicious that Captn. Lewis ment to lead him into an ambuscade with his Enemies. The figure has its right hand on its breast and the left holds the *Calmut* which was given me by Captn. Lewis. In a Tablet I give the Story in a few words, and then add: 'This mantle, composed of 140 Ermine skins was put on Captn. Lewis by *Comehwait*, their Chief. Lewis is supposed to say, Brother, I accept your dress—It is the object of my heart to promote amongst you, our Neighbours, Peace and good will—that you may bury the Hatchet deep in the ground never to be taken up again—and that henceforward you may smoke the *Calmut* of Peace and live in perpetual harmony, not only with each

---

[14] See, e.g., Jackson (1962, No. 171, 1805). In this letter Jefferson, referring to the articles being sent on to Peale, says that he was keeping some specimens for "an Indian Hall I am forming at Monticello, e.g., horns, dressed skins, utensils, etc." This letter also refers to a live magpie and a Columbian Ground Squirrel ("a burrowing squirrel of the prairies," not yet classified at the time) which he is shipping to Peale. In Jackson, Nos. 173 and 177, Peale acknowledges the receipt in good condition of these live animals. Before he moved his Museum, it may be added, Peale kept a sort of menagerie in the yard and stables of his home. In November 1809, writing to his son Rembrandt informing him of Lewis' unexpected death, Peale refers to a consignment of specimens from Lewis himself which had just been received without any accompanying letter (*ibid.*, No. 302). He says these consisted of a collection of "Indian dresses, pipes, arrows, an Indian pot entire, skins of beavers etc., others etc. with some minerals, etc." Since Peale recorded accessions, an entry of December 1809 (*ibid.*, No. 306) provides a detailed inventory of this shipment.

other, but with the white man, your Brothers, who will teach you many useful Arts. Possessed of every comfort in life, what cause ought to involve us in War?' " (Jackson, 1962, No. 281). Peale adds a few homilies in regard to working for amicable relations, and then says: "Such I believe to be the sentiments of our friend Lewis, and which he endeavored to instill in the minds of the various savages he met with in his long and hazardous Tour. I am pleased when ever I can give an object which affords a moral sentiment to the Visitors of the Museum." The general tone of this pseudo address attributed to Lewis is not very far removed from the actual speech which President Jefferson had made to an Osage delegation in Washington a few years before. Referring to the change in sovereignty that had taken place, he said: "Never more will you have occasion to change your fathers. We are all now of one family, born in the same land, and bound to live as brothers; and the strangers from beyond the great water are gone from among us. The Great Spirit has given you strength, and has given us strength; not that we might hurt one another, but to do each other all the good in our power. Our dwellings indeed are very far apart; but not too far to carry on commerce and useful intercourse. You have furs and peltries which we want, and we have clothes and other useful things which you want. Let us employ ourselves then in mutually accomadating each other" (ibid, No. 127).[15]

Insofar as his ethnological collections are concerned, I believe that it is correct to say that Peale's attitude toward them is clearly distinguishable from that exhibited by Du Simitière toward similar material. There seems to be no evidence of even a glimmering of a genuine scientific approach on Peale's part. Peale's collections were eventually dispersed, as Du Simitière's had been, when in the latter case the General Assembly of Pennsylvania refused to purchase and preserve them. What remained of the Lewis and Clark collection ultimately reached the Peabody Museum in Cambridge.[16]

[15] Compare Jefferson's speech to the Osage delegation in Washington (Jackson, 1962, No. 127) and the actual speech of Lewis to the Oto (ibid., No. 129).

[16] Willoughby (1905, p. 634) says that a great deal of the Peale collection passed to the Boston Museum which "in its earlier days was as noted for its cases of wax figures, its ethnological and natural history collections and historical objects as for its theatre." In 1899, however, its collections were dispersed "as gifts among the Museums of Boston and vicinity." The Peabody

Peale is also to be remembered for his portraits of Indians. Joseph Brant (Thayendanegea) was portrayed in 1797 wearing native costume with armband and gorget. Later the Seneca chief Red Jacket, opponent of Christian missions among the Iroquois, sat for both Peale[17] and another Philadelphia painter, John Neagle (1796–1865).[18] The latter painted several portraits of Western Indians when they stopped in Philadelphia en route to Washington. Indeed, some of the best portraits of Indians we have were painted in Philadelphia. Particularly noteworthy are those of the two Lenape Indians who came to Philadelphia to be cheated by John Penn in the notorious "Walking Treaty" of 1735. These were the work of Gustav Hessalius (1682–1755). John Ewers (1949, p. 228) says that they "are the first successful Indian portraits made in North America."[19] Since there was, of course, no photography in those days, to say nothing of anthropometry, and since the artists portrayed their subjects in native costume, these works of art are at the same time documents of prime anthropological value.[20]

As I have pointed out elsewhere, the historical roots of American anthropology were nourished in the "backwash of the frontier," the currents and eddies generated by the contacts between the early settlers and the Indian (Hallowell, 1959, p. 469). After the initial

---

Museum of Harvard received the ethnological collection, including the objects probably collected by Lewis and Clark. One of the most famous surviving objects in the Peabody Museum is a painted Mandan buffalo robe. For a description see Willoughby (p. 638) and a photograph. This robe appears in the invoice of articles forwarded from Fort Mandan to Jefferson in 1805. It is described as "1 Buffalow robe painted by a Mandan man representing a battle which was faught 8 years since, by the Sioux and Ricaras against the Mandans, Minitarras and Ahwahharways" (Jackson, 1962, pp. 235–36). In the same invoice reference is made to "1 earthen pot, such as the Mandans manufacture, and use for culinary purposes." Wedel illustrates two fragmentary Mandan pots which are now to be found in the University Museum (1957, p. 97 and Plate 38). There seems to be little doubt that they came from the Lewis and Clark expedition.

[17] These portraits by Peale are on view in Independence National Historical Park, Philadelphia.

[18] To be found in the Historical Society of Pennsylvania, Philadelphia.

[19] The Hessalius portraits of Tishcohan and Lapowinsa belong to the Historical Society of Pennsylvania.

[20] In 1958 the University Museum assembled an exhibition of paintings of North American Indians, which included the portraits mentioned above.

turmoil of contact had relaxed, the American aborigines aroused an increasing interest on the part of various kinds of learned men, most of whom were under the intellectual spell of the Enlightenment. Various manifestations of this ramified interest in the American Indians constitutes a distinctive part of American culture history. Among other things, it is directly linked with the later development of professional specialization. The men who initially concerned themselves with problems concerning the Indians were anthropologists without portfolios.[21] In its earliest phase American anthropology cannot be dissociated from the studies devoted to the languages, cultures, and physical characteristics of the American Indians by these men, most of whom were associated with the American Philosophical Society. This interest in Indians continued and greatly expanded in the nineteenth century. And it penetrated far beyond the scholarly realm. American dramatists, novelists, and poets became absorbed for a time in the Indian as a subject. In Philadelphia, *Metamora*, or *The Last of the Wampanoags*, was played every year except two for a quarter of a century by Edwin Forrest, the famous Philadelphia actor. In 1828 he had advertised for a play in which "the hero, or principal character, shall be an aboriginal of this country." This play became tremendously popular. It was in Forrest's repertoire for almost forty years. More Americans are said to have seen it in the nineteenth century than attended performances of *Tobacco Road* in the twentieth.[22]

One of the old problems which continued to attract attention

21 In this respect a comparable situation existed in the earliest stages of other disciplines in America, even though in some cases their content had been more exactly defined. Writing about science in general in the days of the early republic, Dupree (1957, p. 7) says: "Science was not separate from philosophy, the arts, or literature in either organization or personnel. Within the framework of natural philosophy and natural history, the particular fields of physics and chemistry, botany, zoology, and mineralogy were clear, but nobody imagined that a man should devote his whole time to one of them. Indeed, almost none of the members [of the American Philosophical Society or the American Academy of Arts and Sciences] were even professional scientists. Many were doctors, lawyers, or clergymen, making their living and spending much of their time in ways unconnected with science." In fact, the term *scientist* was not coined until 1840, when William Whewell deliberately introduced it "to describe a cultivator of science in general" (Bell, p. 8).

22 It was played even after Forrest's death, and a radio version was broadcast in 1939. For further information see Clark (1943).

throughout the last century was the question of Indian origins. In approach and treatment there is a radical antithesis soon to be observed between older writers on this subject and the way the problem is handled after increasing data have accumulated and disciplinary specialization has begun to emerge. William Penn, Quaker founder of Pennsylvania, was among those in a long line of thinkers who believed that the aborigines of this country were descendants of the Lost Tribes of Israel.[23] More than a century later Elias Boudinot (1740–1821), a prominent Philadelphian of his time, expressed similar views. Boudinot had served as president of the Continental Congress. He was a friend of George Washington, who appointed him Director of the Philadelphia Mint. Later he became a trustee of Princeton College. In 1816 he published a book titled *A Star in the West; or, a Humble Attempt to Discover the Long Lost Ten Tribes of Israel, Preparatory to Their Return to Their Beloved City, Jerusalem.* Boudinot's scholarship was in the tradition of the many speculative writers who preceded him. Among other things he converted the Indian war whoop into "Y-O-He-Wah," a corruption of "Jehovah." And he said that the Choctaw Indians intermixed the word "Ha-le-leu-yah" into their lamentations for the dead.[24]

As the nineteenth century wore on speculations of this kind declined, and in Philadelphia there were increasing opportunities for anyone interested to see actual specimens of Indian workmanship, both ethnological and archaeological, as well as some skeletal material. Names now long familiar to all anthropologists begin to crop up. The Academy of Natural Sciences assumed prominence. Flowering from small beginnings in 1812, a large hall was built in 1826 and exhibits and lectures soon became available to the public. Closely associated with the Academy were pioneers in American physical anthropology. Of particular eminence was Samuel G.

[23] For references to the history of this tradition of speculation see Hallowell (1960, pp. 4–6) and Wauchope (1962, Chapter 4 and Bibliography, pp. 142–43).

[24] For further comments on Boudinot, particularly with reference to the speculation of Richard Brothers in England, see Hungerford (1941, pp. 84–85). "The one found in the American Indians the fulfillment of Biblical prophecy; the other found that fulfillment in the English" (described by Brothers as descendants of the Lost Tribes). "Yet so fine a line distinguishes success from failure in scholarship that whereas Richard Brothers, Boudinot's English compeer, was confined to a mad house, Boudinot served as a trustee of Princeton College."

Morton (1799–1851), with whose *Crania Americana* (1839) physical anthropology in the United States may be said to have begun. His famous collection of crania, judged to be the largest in the world at the time, was purchased from his executors after his death and presented to the Academy of Natural Sciences. Other men associated with this institution whose contributions to physical anthropology are a matter of record were: J. Aitken Meigs (1829–1879), author of an early detailed article (1861) on 48 cranial measurements and determinations that should be taken on the skull; Joseph Leidy (1823–1891), and Harrison Allen (1841–1897). Meigs was made a Foreign Associate Member of the Anthropological Society of Paris in 1860, and an Honorary Fellow of the Anthropological Society of London in 1863.[25]

Archaeological and ethnological collections were also acquired by the Academy; the Haldeman collection of New World material, which included specimens from Middle and South America, the superb archaeological material from the Southern United States excavated by Clarence B. Moore, and the Vaux collection of archaeological material from Europe (Mitra, 1933, pp. 185–86). When the Academy celebrated its 125th Anniversary in 1937, the major feature was an international symposium on early man. It was organized by Edgar B. Howard, who had studied anthropology and geology at the University of Pennsylvania.[26] This conference was attended by scholars from all over the world. V. Gordon Childe, Kaj Birket-Smith, and Dorothy A. E. Garrod received honorary degrees of Doctor of Science from the University of Pennsylvania at this time at a special convocation held in the auditorium of its Museum. This celebration actually marked the heyday of the Academy's anthropological interests.

In the field of medicine, the assembly of skeletal material and prep-

[25] For the bibliographies of these men and biographical details, see Hrdlička (1919). See Brinton (1897) for a review of Allen's work. For the position of Morton and other Philadelphians in the polygenist-monogenist controversy, see Stanton (1960).

[26] He received his Master's degree in the Department of Anthropology and his doctorate in the Department of Geology (1935). For additional information see the *Obituary* by J. Alden Mason (1942b). Thirty-six papers presented at the symposium were collected and published in March 1937, edited by George Grant MacCurdy (MacCurdy 1937).

arations of anatomical interest, without the concentration upon crania which typified physical anthropology at an early stage, had attracted the attention of physicians even earlier. In Philadelphia, this interest was pursued by Dr. Caspar Wistar (1761–1818), who belonged to an earlier generation than Morton. It culminated in a more fully ramified biological context, including comparative anatomy and physical anthropology, with the foundation of the Wistar Institute of Anatomy and Biology seventy years ago.

Caspar Wistar, having secured his medical degree from the University of Pennsylvania in 1782, continued his studies abroad. Inspired by the example of John Hunter (1728–1793), whose collection became the nucleus of the world-famous Hunterian Museum in London, Wistar began to assemble his own anatomical collection. Returning to the United States, he became professor of anatomy at his alma mater in 1808. Wistar was one of the Philadelphia physicians consulted by Jefferson when the Lewis and Clark expedition was being planned, and in 1815 he became Jefferson's successor as President of the American Philosophical Society. His collection was presented by his widow to the University. It was fostered and augmented by Dr. William E. Horner, who had long been his assistant and colleague, and later by Dr. Joseph Leidy. When Provost William Pepper, also a physician, promoted the foundation of the Wistar Institute, incorporated in 1892, the University of Pennsylvania contributed the Wistar-Horner anatomical collection and the land for a building.[27] Dr. Pepper was the first President of the Institute, and Dr. Harrison Allen, a pioneer physical anthropologist, became its first Director. The latter completed his pioneer work on Hawaiian skulls just before his death in 1897.

In this century the Institute became enriched by additional collections, including osteological material that had been housed in the University Museum until 1915; it became famous for its collection of the brains of distinguished men and the work done in comparative anatomy by Henry H. Donaldson (1857–1938), whose book on the *Growth of the Brain* (1897) was a pioneer work. Among other

[27] For information on Dr. Caspar Wistar and the foundation of the Institute, see *Proceedings* (1900, pp. 153–54). For additional information on the Institute, H. H. Donaldson, Ralph Linton, and Ernest W. Hawkes, see Hrdlička, pp. 110–11).

material, an important series of Eskimo crania and other skeletal material had been acquired, which was studied by both Ralph Linton and Ernest W. Hawkes. The latter, who was the first to receive his Doctor's degree (1915) after a Department of Anthropology had been organized here, made observations and measurements on this collection the subject of his dissertation. Besides this, the Wistar Institute became the publisher of the *American Journal of Physical Anthropology*, founded by Hrdlička in 1918, many years before the American Association of Physical Anthropologists was itself organized.

In addition to being the locale of expanding anthropological collections of many different kinds during the last century, Philadelphians also had the opportunity of seeing special visiting exhibits. George Catlin brought his Indian Gallery here before he took it to Europe in 1839. It comprised almost 500 paintings of Indians and Indian life, besides specimens of clothing and handicrafts. As Ewers says: "No one had brought the Wild West to civilization in pictorial form for everyone to see before" (Ewers, 1956, p. 502). The *Philadelphia Saturday Courier* (1838) said: "There is not in our land, nor in any part of Europe . . . anything of the kind more extraordinary or more interesting" (McCracken, p. 188). Catlin was no stranger to Philadelphia. Pennsylvania-born, and raised in the Wyoming Valley, he moved to Philadelphia in order to devote his full time to painting after briefly practicing law for a few years. In 1824 he was elected an academician of the Pennsylvania Academy of Fine Arts, which included among its members Charles Willson Peale. It was in this same year, too, that Catlin had his first glimpse of Western Indians, a delegation en route to Washington having stopped for a few days in Philadelphia. Of this event, which imbued him with the inspiration for his life's work, he later wrote:

My mind was continually reaching for some branch or enterprise of the art, on which to devote a whole life-time of enthusiasm; when a delegation of some ten or fifteen noble and dignified looking Indians, from the wilds of the 'Far West,' suddenly arrived in the city for a few days, arrayed in all their classic beauty—with shield and helmet,—with tunic and manteau,—tinted and tassled off, exactly for the painter's pallette! In silent and stoic dignity, these lords of the forest strutted about the city for a few days, wrapped in their pictured robes, with their brows plumed with the quills of the war-eagle, attracting the attention of all who beheld them. After this they took their leave for Washington City, and I was left to reflect and regret, which I did long and deeply, until I came to the following deductions and conclusions.... Man, in the simplicity and loftiness of his nature, unrestrained and un-fettered by the disguises of art, is surely the most beautiful model for the painter,—and the country from which he hails is unquestionably the best study or school of the arts in the world; such I am sure, from the models I have seen, is the wilderness of North America. And the history and customs of such a people, preserved by pictorial illustrations, are themes worthy the life-time of one man, and nothing short of the loss of my life shall prevent me from visiting their country, and becom-ing their historian. . . . I set out on my arduous and perilous undertaking with the determination of reaching, ultimately, every tribe of Indians on the Continent of North America, and of bringing home faithful portraits of their principal personages, both men and women, from each tribe, views of their villages, games, etc. and full notes on their character and history. I designed, also, to procure their costumes, and a complete collection of their manufactures and weapons, and to perpetuate them in a *Gallery unique,* for the use and instruction of future ages (Catlin, 1841, Vol. 1, pp. 2–3).

Since Catlin was familiar with Peale's Museum, it seems likely that the plan of Peale's exhibition rooms was an important element in his determination to present his Indian paintings, along with relevant ethnographic collections, in the form of the unique gallery to which he refers.

As in other parts of the country, the mysterious Mound Builders aroused tremendous popular interest here in the early decades of the last century.[28] One Philadelphian who became actively interested in excavation was Dr. Montroville Wilson Dickerson (1810–1882), who spent several years traveling and digging in the Mississippi Valley. As a consequence, Dr. Dickerson designed a panorama which was exhibited together with his collection around the middle of the century in Philadelphia and elsewhere. The panorama was advertised as covering more than 15,000 square feet of canvas, al-though in reality we now know that it only covered about 2,500 square feet, because Dr. Mason measured it. As the panorama un-rolled, the spectator saw the burial of De Soto, the effects of the

[28] See Hallowell (1960, pp. 74–85) for further information and references.

great tornado of 1844, and scenes of the mounds and earthworks of the Middle West in their excavated and unexcavated state. Among the mound groups delineated were those at Marietta, Circleville, Portsmouth, Bon Hom Island, Baluxie, and Lake Concordia. This panorama was acquired by the University Museum in 1899. It was last shown in 1941, at a meeting of the Eastern States Archaeological Federation.[29]

One of the great events of nineteenth-century Philadelphia was the Centennial Exposition in 1876. At this time the Indian Bureau of the Department of the Interior and the Smithsonian Institution collected material for a joint display of the ethnology and archaeology of the United States (Ewers, 1959).[30] At this exposition, objects from the mounds already made famous by Squier and Davis in their *Ancient Monuments of the Mississippi Valley* (1848) could be seen at first hand. Frank Hamilton Cushing (1857–1900), then a young man of nineteen, might be said to have been a living part of the ethnological exhibits. He edified the public by his remarkable talent for imitating Indian handicrafts of all kinds. For he had mastered the art of stone chipping, pottery and basket making, weaving and skin-dressing. It was not until after this that Major Powell gave him a job at the Bureau of American Ethnology, which led to his sojourn in the Southwest, where he lived as an adopted Zuñi from 1879–1884 (Cushing, 1920). Returning to Philadelphia in the mid-nineties, Cushing had his portrait, in Zuñi costume painted by the great Thomas Eakins in his studio on Chestnut Street. Cushing is seen wearing a buckskin suit with many necklaces of turquoise and a turquoise in his large earring. Hanging on the wall behind him are a

[29] For additional information see Mason, 1942a. The Dickerson archaeological collections were exhibited in Philadelphia in 1867 and again at the Centennial Exposition a decade later. After this they were transferred to Memorial Hall in Fairmount Park, where they remained until 1885, "Soon thereafter," Mason says, "they were acquired by the Department of Archaelogy and Paleontology of the University of Pennsylvania, which later became the University Museum." The diorama was exhibited by the Art Museum of St. Louis in 1949 and later acquired by that museum. See also McDermott (1958, pp. 170–72).

[30] A special appropriation for this display was obtained, and collecting was mainly confined to "those parts of the United States which were not already properly represented" since, after the Exposition closed, the specimens were to be transferred to the Smithsonian.

number of Zuñi objects. A piece of turreted pottery stands on a slab above a fire at the lower right. Cushing proved that he had not lost his talent for handicrafts by making a pair of moccasins for the artist.[31] Cushing's classic paper on copper working appeared later (1894), and the stunning wooden sculptures and other objects of the Key Marco culture he excavated are among the prize exhibits of the University Museum.

Beginning with the eighties, we enter a new era. We see the establishment of archaeological collections at the University of Pennsylvania, along with a concomitant program of research. And we see the emergence of Daniel G. Brinton (1837–1899) as a leader in the promotion of anthropology as an academic discipline, conceived in essentially the same inclusive terms in which we view the subject today.

The archaeological collections marked the beginning of what later became the University Museum, which celebrated its 75th anniversary in 1962.[32] I need not go into a history of the Museum in any detail here, since Percy C. Madeira Jr., has written one (1964). Suffice it to say that, beginning with a small collection of objects donated to the University in the eighties, Provost William Pepper (1843–1898) established a museum of archaeology and paleontology in the old library building soon after its completion in 1889. The collection remained there until the University Museum building was completed a decade later. Stewart Culin (1858–1929), of later game fame, was director of this collection during this period. Concur-

---

[31] This portrait is to be found in the Thomas Gilcrease Institute of American History and Art, Tulsa, Oklahoma. A photograph is included in Porter (1959, Plate 47).

[32] On this occasion J. Eric S. Thompson (Faculty Board of Archaeology, Cambridge University) gave the Convocation Address and was awarded an Honorary Degree (J. E. S. Thompson, 1962). In an article describing "The Department of Archaeology" (1892b) seventy years before (1892) Brinton refers to an American section, an Assyrian section, an Egyptian section, etc. "By the 1st of April 1891," he says (p. 378) "there were nearly 10,000 entries in the American department of the Museum, representing about 30,000 objects, besides material which was still on hand, but at that date not entered in the catalogue." The United States, he says, is represented by objects from thirty-six states and six territories and, outside this area, there are specimens from Canada, the West Indies, New Zealand, Samoa, Fiji, the New Hebrides, the Solomon Islands, Torres Straits, and Australia. Several boxes of remains of the Swiss Lake Dwellers were also included in the collection at this time.

rently, Pepper founded an archaeological association, the purpose of which was to provide funds, independently of the University, for the promotion of archaeological research and publication. Mrs. Phoebe Hearst, whose later patronage of anthropology at the University of California is familiar, was an active member for a time of the archaeological association organized and led by Dr. Pepper.

About the same time Provost Pepper, hearing about a projected expedition to southern Iraq, worked out an arrangement which led to excavations at Nippur under the auspices of the University. Beginning in 1888, thousands of cuneiform tablets from the Temple Library were recovered in a series of pioneer expeditions. In 1891, Dr. Pepper created the Department of Archaeology and Paleontology, which he directed after his resignation as Provost in 1894. He likewise promoted the erection of the building which became the present University Museum. It has been called "the last creation of Dr. Pepper's genius," but he did not live to enter it. As a consequence of his far-flung archaeological interests, Pepper also served a term as President of the Pennsylvania branch of the Archaeological Institute of America, which had been founded in 1879 (*Proceedings*, 1900, pp. 159–63). This organization, from the start, gave recognition to American as well as Old World archaeology. F. W. Putnam was active in its formation, and Lewis H. Morgan was asked to prepare a plan of research in the American field (White, 1942, pp. 1–2). Thus Dr. Pepper, although not an archaeologist himself, was actively in touch for a decade with current developments everywhere in this field, and devoted himself in particular to the promotion of research under University auspices. It was he who, learning of the archaeological work already done by Max Uhle, secured his services for the famous dig at the Temple of Pachacamac in Peru (1895–1896). This was the scene, says Mason, "of the first scientific archaeological work in Peru" (J. A. Mason, 1957, p. 100).[33] Cushing's

[33] For additional information on Uhle see Rowe (1954). The latter says (p. 1) that "when Uhle started work, American Archaeology was wholly without depth. A good deal of digging and collecting had been done and local styles were fairly well known in some areas, but American antiquities were all simply 'pre-Columbian.' It was Uhle who first applied modern principles of stratigraphy and seriation to American materials and sorted them out into a chronological sequence. This is only part of his achievement, but it is probably the part that will be longest remembered." For the more explicit circumstances under which Uhle was brought to Philadelphia and those which later lured

excavations in Florida were also promoted by Pepper during this period, in support of which the aid of Mrs. Hearst was obtained.[34] Daniel G. Brinton, only a few years older than William Pepper was also a physician by training, receiving his M.D. from Jefferson Medical College in 1861. But the years he spent in private practice were few.[35] He was a man with the widest intellectual interests, and a prolific writer besides. Among other things, he published on the poetry of Whitman and Browning as well as in the medical field. In anthropology he dealt with somatological, archaeological, ethnographical, and linguistic data. He ranged far beyond the American Indian, although he is best known, perhaps, for work in this area, particularly in linguistics and mythology.[36] Brinton was very active in the American Philosophical Society, as John Freeman points out in these proceedings, and in 1884 he was made Professor of Ethnology and Archaeology in the Academy of Natural Sciences. Two years later he became Professor of American Linguistics and Archaeology at the University of Pennsylvania, a position which, while a signal honor, carried no pecuniary rewards for the incumbent.

---

him to the University of California, see pp. 4, 6. It appears that it was Pepper's death in 1898 which was the major factor which led Uhle to accept an offer from California. Mrs. Phoebe Hearst, who became his patron there, was a close friend of Pepper and shared the latter's interest in archaeology, as we have indicated.

[34] These excavations were sometimes referred to as the Pepper-Hearst Expedition. It should be noted that under the provostship of William Pepper (1881–1894), the University underwent a phenomenal expansion and achieved a national recognition. The faculty was trebled, attendance increased from 800 to almost 3,000, more than a dozen new departments were created, and there was a large increase in endowments. See, e.g., Thorpe's biography of Pepper (1904, p. 458).

[35] In 1862, returning from a year's study abroad, he joined the Medical Corps of the Union army, and was not discharged until 1865. In 1867 he became assistant editor of the *Medical and Surgical Reporter;* in 1874 he was made editor, and held this position until 1887. His published writings include 23 books and more than 200 articles.

[36] Stewart Culin prepared a bibliography for the memorial meeting held under the auspices of the American Philosophical Society (*Proceedings,* 1900, pp. 42–67); a selected bibliography, broadly relevant to physical anthropology, is to be found in Hrdlička (1919, pp. 63–64); and in his obituary notice Chamberlain lists publications "dealing more or less directly with Folk-Lore, Mythology, and allied topics."

By this time Brinton's work in American linguistics was internationally known. Besides many articles, he had initiated his unique *Library of Aboriginal American Literature* (1882), each volume of which comprised "a work composed in a native tongue by a native," with notes, glosses and other sections designed to make the text intelligible to the student.[37] In 1886, he was the first American to receive the medal of the Société Américaine de France for his "numerous and learned works on American Ethnology." While never a field archaeologist, Brinton was nevertheless erudite in this area also. In 1883 the article "American Archaeology" in the American Supplement to the *Encyclopaedia Britannica* was written by him, and both hemispheres were covered in a 116-page article on "Prehistoric Archeology" which Brinton contributed to the *Iconographic Encyclopaedia* in 1886. In the field of American archaeology Brinton was among the first (1866) to argue, on the basis of documentary evidence, that the Mound Builders were Indians, related to historic tribes, and not an alien or mysterious people. This article long antedated the "modern" period in mound archaeology, which culminated in the report of Cyrus Thomas in 1894 (Brinton, 1881).[38]

At the University, Brinton taught courses which were limited to graduate students. In content they included, among other things: methods of archaeological exploration, the characteristics of the remains of different archaeological provinces in North and South America, the structure of American Indian languages and the characteristics of different linguistic stocks, the relations of archaeology to ethnography, and the evolution of religion.

Despite the fact that in formal terms his offerings were never labeled anthropology, there is ample evidence to show that Dr. Brinton looked upon himself as an anthropologist in the inclusive sense in which that term was already being used in the United States, and that his contemporaries were aware of this fact and placed him in this category. In 1891, for example, Otis T. Mason in a review of Brinton's book *Races and Peoples*, took particular notice of the

[37] At the suggestion of the bibliographer J. C. Pilling, Brinton prepared a list of his publications in the field of American linguistics. This was privately printed and circulated in 1898 under the title *A Record of Study in Aboriginal American Languages*. There are 15 general articles and books listed; 14 items deal with languages north of Mexico, 31 with the Indian languages of Mexico and Central America, and 16 with those of the West Indies and South America.

[38] For the Mound Builders as a problem, see Hallowell (1960, pp. 75–81).

author's appointment to the faculty of the University and said: "If we are not mistaken this is the first attempt by an institution of higher learning in our country to found a professorship of anthropology" (O. T. Mason, 1891). Brinton's identification as an anthropologist becomes even more apparent when we turn to the phrasing of the addresses of speakers at the Memorial Meeting held in January 1900, six months after his death.

Provost Charles Custis Harrison, who presided at this meeting, although referring to Brinton's chair by title, goes on to say that his "devotion to what he himself called 'the new science of anthropology' was most interesting. He had the utmost confidence, not only in the importance of the science itself as a science, but also in its practical value as an applied science in politics, education and legislation. He was not in any way a mere 'collector' or 'observer' in the familiar sense of these words." (*Proceedings*, 1900, pp. 216–17). On the same occasion, F. W. Putnam (1839–1915), a contemporary of Brinton, whose activies as a promoter in the general field of anthropology had ranged far and wide, was present. At the time he was Professor of American Archaeology and Ethnology at Harvard, and like Brinton he had been the recipient of the degree of Doctor of Science from the University of Pennsylvania during the previous decade. At the Memorial Meeting he represented the American Association for the Advancement of Science, which he had served as Permanent Secretary for twenty-five years, and as President in 1898. In the course of his remarks, he said that a fitting memorial to Brinton on the part of the University would be the establishment, not of a chair of archaeology as the Provost had suggested, but rather of a professorship of anthropology. He went on to say that this would give "further aid and encouragement to that branch of American science which he loved so well and worked so earnestly to advance," and that it would likewise "meet with the hearty approval and coöperation of all workers in anthropology throughout the country" (*ibid.*, p. 239).

What I wish to emphasize particularly is the fact that in this country Brinton was the pioneer in teaching anthropology [39] (De

[39] In 1906 the greater part of one issue of the *American Anthropologist* (n.s., Vol. 8, No. 3) was devoted to "Recent Progress in American Anthropology. A Review of the Activities of Institutions and Individuals from 1902 to 1906." In the section devoted to the University of Pennsylvania (pp. 479–83) it is

Laguna, 1960, p. 102), that the nomenclature suggested in his article of 1892 prevailed,[40] and that he was first and last an active promoter of anthropology as an autonomous academic discipline, including a program of gruaduate work leading to the doctorate. In the Prefatory Note to a pamphlet privately printed and circulated in 1892 and bearing the title *Anthropology, as a Science and as a Branch of University Education in the U.S.*, Brinton says: "the rightful claims of this science will be recognized only when it is organized as a department by itself, with a competent corps of professors and docents, with well-appointed laboratories and museums, and with fellowships for deserving students." On June 2 of the same year he wrote to Provost William Pepper making "some suggestions for establishing instruction in the science of anthropology in the University, to form a constituent part of the branches eligible for the degree of Ph.D." He reviewed the precedents for such instruction both in faculty and personnel and in research materials which, he believed, would make possible the implementation of his proposal.[41]

---

stated (p. 482) that "when in 1886 Dr. Brinton was appointed to the chair of American Archaeology and Linguistics at the University of Pennsylvania, that institution took the initial step in a movement which, taken up soon afterward by Harvard, has led to the introduction of anthropology as a distinct branch of learning into all the principal universities in the United States. In founding a chair of American Archaeology and Ethnology [sic], Pennsylvania was not only the first of American universities to recognize the claim of these special branches of investigation, but was the first to introduce the study of anthropology as a distinct science. It is well known that Dr. Brinton's comprehensive exposition of his subject embraced the whole science of anthropology, and his lectures foreshadowed the later development of instruction in anthropology in America. Although first in this movement, the University of Pennsylvania did not subsequently make so rapid progress in this particular direction as some of the other American universities. In recent years, however, there has been renewed activity in this respect."

[40] This article, an abstract of an address delivered before the Anthropological Society of Washington in April, was published in the *American Anthropologist* in July 1892 and is reprinted in DeLaguna (1960). The terminology and content of the subject had been under considerable discussion by this time, and J. W. Powell, who had developed a special terminology of his own, commented on Brinton's paper. It is interesting, as DeLaguna says (p. 99), "that Brinton's taxonomy has won out in the long run, despite Powell's great prestige as director of the Bureau of Ethnology."

[41] Here I am indebted to Professor Leonidas Dodson, Archivist of the University of Pennsylvania, since I have not seen the letter cited referred to elsewhere.

His suggestion, however, did not lead to any action at the time. But it was in the same year that Brinton was invited to examine the first person to receive a Ph.D. in Anthropology at an American university. The candidate was Alexander Francis Chamberlain (1865–1914) at Clark University (Chamberlain, 1900, pp. 219, 220). While there was no anthropology department there, it will be recalled that G. Stanley Hall brought Franz Boas to Clark in 1889 where he taught for three years. But since no department was organized, the program so boldly initiated did not flourish.[42]

After his death, Brinton's library passed to the University Museum, where it is still housed. On May 13, 1937, the centenary of his birth was celebrated at the Delaware County Institute of Science in Media, Pennsylvania. Brinton had been an active member of the Institute when he made his home in Media in his later years. Delegates from many learned societies attended, and they were addressed by Edwin C. Conklin and Clark Wissler (J. A. Mason, 1938). In 1942 the Philadelphia Anthropological Society initiated a series of monographs dedicated to Brinton's memory. These publications were largely made possible through contributions from his heirs.

Although Brinton had initiated the teaching of anthropology at the University, his major influence was exerted more widely through his writings and activities elsewhere,[43] since no organized academic program was developed under his direction. And following his death there was no one of equal anthropological distinction available on the local scene. Stewart Culin, who remained in Philadelphia until 1903, when he joined the staff of the Brooklyn Museum, offered some courses in the University Museum between 1900 and 1902. However, the first undergraduate courses *listed* as anthropology, were given by George Byron Gordon (1870–1927), who became Curator of Anthropology in 1904, and later Director of the Museum. It was not until Frank G. Speck arrived in 1907 that a more fully rounded program began to emerge, including the intro-

[42] George A. Dorsey, who received his Ph.D. from Harvard University in 1894, was the first to acquire a doctorate from a university in the United States in which there was a formally organized department of anthropology.

[43] He was, for example, President of the World's Fair Congress of Anthropology held in conjunction with the Columbia Exposition in Chicago, 1893, making the opening address. See DeLaguna (1960, pp. 423–34). In 1894 Brinton served as President of the AAAS, a distinction he shared with three other nineteenth-century anthropologists: Morgan, Powell, and Putnam.

duction of graduate instruction leading to a doctorate, thus bringing
to delayed fruition Brinton's recommendations of 1892.[44]

Frank G. Speck had studied at Columbia University under Franz
Boas, but in 1908 was awarded the first Ph.D. in Anthropology at
Pennsylvania. His thesis, "The Ethnology of the Yuchi Indians,"
was published as the initial volume in the newly established Anthropological Publications of the University of Pennsylvania Museum
(1909). Speck organized the Department of Anthropology in 1910,
and for several years thereafter courses continued to be given
within the Museum walls, as they had previously. The lecture hall
used for larger classes was the Widener Auditorium, which was
remodeled in 1961 into the offices now occupied by the Anthropology Department. I am sometimes surprised to find myself sitting in
the balcony of this old lecture hall. For that is where my office is. It
was from the floor of this same lecture hall that as an undergraduate
I first heard Frank Speck address his class in Anthropology I, although I was not enrolled in it. At that time I had not the faintest
notion that I should ever become an anthropologist. Nor did I antic-
ipate the fact that Frank and I would become intimate friends, that
he would be my mentor in anthropology, and that we would become so closely associated in the department for many years.

I trust that the odd bits of historical information that I have
patched together suggest some kind of underlying continuity, or
even cumulative trends, in the history of anthropology in Phila-

[44] J. Alden Mason (1950a), who was graduated from the University of
Pennsylvania in 1907, has provided some recollections of this period: "Well I
remember the supplementary sheet in the catalogue of 1903-4 in my freshman
year. Among other 'Special Announcements' it stated that beginning in 1904–
5, elective courses would be given in anthropology. There were two one-
semester courses that first year; 701, General Anthropology, and 702, American
Archeology and Ethnology. In 1905-6, General Anthropology was enlarged to
a full year course, and 703, Ethnology of Europe, replaced it as a one-semester
course." Mason pursued graduate work there after 1907, taking some courses
with Speck after the latter arrived on the scene. "The year 1909–10 was a
productive one at Pennsylvania for anthropologists," Mason goes on to say.
"Both Frank G. Speck and Edward Sapir taught full time, with G. B. Gordon
teaching part time. I again held a scholarship, a full-time one this year and
profited greatly. At the end of that year Sapir went to head the Anthropology
Department of the Geological Survey of Canada and I went to California for
more graduate work [with Kroeber], not to return to Pennsylvania until
1926."

delphia. I believe that further research in depth, including the correspondence of important figures, would reveal connecting links and developmental sequences more clearly. But this remains for the future. Anthropology at large has not yet developed an acute historical consciousness. As I see it, the history of anthropology in Philadelphia is only a small segment of a larger whole. I hope I have said enough, however, to indicate that anthropological activities here, when viewed in historical perspective, have been an integral part of a wider flow of events elsewhere and have influenced them as well. Awareness of past events should lead to a more rational appraisal of contemporary aims and achievements, as well as a sounder evaluation of our future goals and the best means to achieve them.

REFERENCES

Bell, Whitfield J., Jr. (1955). *Early American Science: Needs and Opportunities for Study*. Williamsburg, Va., Institute of Early American History and Culture.

Biddle, Nicholas (1814). *History of the expedition under the command of Captains Lewis and Clark, to the sources of the Missouri, thence across the Rocky Mountains and down the River Columbia to the Pacific Ocean. Performed during the years 1804–5–6. By order of the government of the United States*. Prepared for the press by Paul Allen. 2 vol. Philadelphia, Bradford and Inkeep.

Boudinot, Elias (1816). *A star in the West; or, a Humble Attempt to Discover the Long Lost Ten Tribes of Israel, Preparatory to the Return to their Beloved City, Jerusalem*. Trenton, N.J., D. Fenton, S. Hutchinson, and J. Dunham.

Bridenbaugh, Carl and Jessica (1942). *Rebels and Gentlemen. Philadelphia in the Age of Franklin*. New York, Reynal and Hitchcock (Reissued as a paperback, 1962).

Brinton, Daniel G. (1866). "The Mound-builders of the Mississippi Valley," *Historical Magazine*, 11, pp. 33–37.

———(1881). "The Probable Nationality of the Mound-builders," *American Antiquarian*, 4, pp. 9–18.

———(1883). "American Archaeology," *Encyclopaedia Britannica*, American Supplement, 1, pp. 278–86.

———(1886). "Prehistoric Archaeology," *Iconographic Encyclopaedia*, 2, p. 16

28   A. IRVING HALLOWELL

———(1892a). *Anthropology, as a Science and as a Branch of University Education in the United States.* Privately printed.

———(1892b). "The Department of Archaeology," in *Benjamin Franklin and the University of Pennsylvania.*, ed. by Francis Newton Thrope. Washington, D.C., Bureau of Education, 1893.

———(1892c). "The Nomenclature and Teaching of Anthropology," *American Anthropologist* 5, pp. 263–71. (Reprinted in De Laguna).

———(1895). "The Aims of Anthropology," American Association for the Advancement of Science, 44, *Proceedings*, pp. 1–17.

———(1897). "Dr. Allen's Contributions to Anthropology," American Academy of Natural Sciences of Philadelphia, 46, *Proceedings*, pp. 522–29.

Brinton, Daniel G. (1898). *A Record of Study in American Aboriginal Languages.* Media, Pa., privately printed.

Catlin, George (1841). *Letters and Notes on the Manners, Customs, and Conditions of the North American Indians.* 2 vol. London, published by the author at Egyptian Hall, Piccadilly.

Chamberlain, Alexander F. (1900). "In Memoriam: Daniel Garrison Brinton," *Journal of American Folklore*, 12, pp. 215–25.

Chinard, Gilbert (1943). "Jefferson and the American Philosophical Society," American Philosophical Society, 87, *Proceedings*, pp. 263–76.

Clark, Barrett H. (ed.) (1943). *Favorite American Plays of the Nineteenth Century.* Princeton, Princeton University Press.

Colton, Harold S. (1909). "Peale's Museum," *Popular Science Monthly*, 75, pp. 221–38.

Cushing, Frank Hamilton (1894). "Primitive Copper Working; An Experimental Study," *American Anthropologist*, 7, pp. 93–117.

———(1896). "Preliminary Report on the Exploration of Ancient Key Dwellers' Remains on the Gulf Coast of Florida," American Philosophical Society, 35, *Proceedings*, pp. 329–432.

———(1920). *Zuni Breadstuff.* Indian Notes and Monographs 8, New York, Museum of the American Indian, Heye Foundation.

De Laguna, Frederica (ed.) (1960). *Selected Papers from the American Anthropologist, 1888–1920.* New York, Harper and Row.

De Voto, Bernard (1953). *The Journals of Lewis and Clark.* Boston, Houghton Mifflin.

Dupree, A. Hunter (1957). *Science in the Federal Government.* Cambridge, Belnap Press of Harvard University.

Ewers, John C. (1949). "An Anthropologist Looks at Early Pictures of North American Indians," *New York Historical Society Quarterly*, 33, pp. 222–35.

——(1956). "George Catlin, Painter of Indians and the West," *Annual Report of the Smithsonian Institution for 1955.* Washington, pp. 483–506.

——(1959). "A Century of American Indian Exhibits in the Smithsonian Institution," *Annual Report of the Smithsonian Institution for 1958.* pp. 513–52.

Greene, John C. (1960). "Early Scientific Interest in the American Indian: Comparative Linguistics," American Philosophical Society, *Proceedings,* 104, pp. 511–17.

Hallowell, A. Irving (1957). "The Backwash of the Frontier: The Impact of the Indian on American Culture," *Annual Report of the Smithsonian Institution for 1958,* pp. 447–72. Washington, 1959. (This article is reprinted from *The Frontier in Perspective,* ed. by Walker D. Wyman and Clifton B. Kroeber. Madison, University of Wisconson Press, 1957. The Smithsonian reprinting contains 8 plates not in the original.)

——(1960). "The Beginnings of Anthropology in America," in Frederica De Laguna (ed.), *Selected Papers from the American Anthropologist, 1888–1920,* New York, Harper and Row, pp. 1–90.

Hrdlička, Ales (1919). *Physical Anthropology: Its Scope and Aims; Its History and Present Status in the United States.* Philadelphia, Wistar Institute of Anatomy and Biology.

Hungerford, E. B. (1941). *Shores of Darkness.* New York, Columbia University Press.

Huth, Hans (1945). "Pierre Eugene DuSimitière and the Beginnings of the American Historical Museum," *Pennsylvania Magazine of History,* 69, pp. 315–25.

Jackson, Donald (ed.) (1962). *Letters of the Lewis and Clark Expedition with Related Documents 1783–1854.* Urbana, University of Illinois Press.

Kroeber, Theodora (1961). *Ishi in Two Worlds: A Biography of the Last Wild Indian in North America.* Berkeley and Los Angeles, University of California Press.

Levey, Martin (1951). "The First American Museum of Natural History," *Isis,* 42, pp. 10–12.

Lurie, Nancy Oestreich (1966). "Women in Early American Anthropology," in June Helm (ed.), *Pioneers of American Anthropology* (Seattle, University of Washington Press), pp. 31–81.

McCracken, Harold (1959). *George Catlin and the Old Frontier.* New York, Dial Press.

MacCurdy, George Grant (ed.) (1937). *Early Man, as Depicted by*

30   A. IRVING HALLOWELL

Leading Authorities at the International Symposium, the Academy of
Natural Sciences, Philadelphia, March 1937. Philadelphia, Lippincott.
McDermott, John Francis (1958). The Lost Panoramas of the Mississippi.
Chicago, University of Chicago Press, pp. 170–72.
McHenry, Margaret (1946). Thomas Eakins who Painted. Privately
printed.
Madeira, Percy (1964). Man in Search of Man. Philadelphia, University
of Pennsylvania.
Mason, J. Alden (1938). "Brinton Anniversary," Journal of American
Folklore 51, pp. 106–7.
———(1942a). "Grand Moving Diorama, a Special Feature," The
Pennsylvania Archaeologist 12 (1942), No. 1, pp. 14–16. [Reprinted in
Minnesota History, 23 (1942), pp. 352–54.]
———(1942b). "Obituary of Edgar B. Howard," American Antiquity,
9, pp. 230–34.
———(1950a). "Frank Gouldsmith Speck, 1881–1950," Philadelphia
Anthropological Society, Bulletin, 3, No. 4. (Obituary notice.)
———(1950b). "The Beginnings of Anthropology at the University of
Pennsylvania," Philadelphia Anthropological Society, Bulletin, No. 3.
———(1950c). "Frank Gouldsmith Speck, 1881–1950." University
Museum Bulletin 15, No. 1, pp. 3–5. With photograph of Speck. This
number contains Frank G. Speck, "Concerning Iconology and the
Masking Complex in Eastern North America," p. 6–57.
———(1957). The Ancient Civilizations of Peru. Penguin Books.
Mason, Otis T. (1891). "Review of D. G. Brinton's 'Races and Peoples,'" American Anthropologist, 4, pp. 68–88.
Mitra, Panchanan (1933). A History of American Anthropology. Uni-
versity of Calcutta.
The Noble Savage, The American Indian in Art, with an introduction
by Robert C. Smith. (Exhibition at the University Museum, 1958).
Pennsylvania Historical Records Survey (1940). Descriptive Catalogue
of the DuSimitière Papers in the Library Company of Philadelphia.
Porter, Fairfield (1959). Thomas Eakins. New York, George Braziller,
1959 (Great American Artists series).
Potts, William J. (1889). "DuSimitière, Artist, Antiquary, and Naturalist,
Projector of the First American Museum with some Extracts from his
Notebook," Pennsylvania Magazine of History, 13, pp. 341–75.
"Recent Progress in American Anthropology. A Review of the Activities
of Institutions and Individuals from 1902–1906. Presented to the Fif-
teenth International Congress of Americanists, Quebec. 1906," American Anthropologists, 1906, N.S. 8, No. 3, pp. 441–558.

Proceedings, American Philosophical Society. (1900). Memorial Volume 1.

Rowe, John Howland (1954). "Max Uhle, 1856–1944. A Memoir of the Father of Peruvian Archaeology," *University of California Publications in American Archaeology and Ethnography,* 46, No. 1, pp. 1–134, plates 1–14. Berkeley and Los Angeles.

Simpson, George G. (1942). "The First Natural History Museum in America," *Science,* 96, pp. 261–63.

Stanton, William (1960). *The Leopard's Spots. Scientific Attitudes toward Race in America, 1815–1859.* Chicago, University of Chicago Press.

Thomas, Cyrus (1894). "Report on the Mound Explorations of the Bureau of American Ethnology," Bureau of American Ethnology, 12th Annual Report, 1890–91, pp. 27–730.

Thompson, J. Eric S. (1962). "Convocation Address," *Expedition,* 4, No. 3, pp. 14–16.

Thorpe, Francis Newton (1904). *William Pepper.* Philadelphia, Lippincott.

Thwaites, Reuben Gold, ed. (1904–5) *Original Journals of the Lewis and Clark Expedition, 1804–1806, printed from the original manuscript in the library of the American Philosophical Society and by direction of its committee on historical documents, together with manuscript material of Lewis and Clark from other sources . . . now for the first time published in full and exactly as written.* 8 vols. (New York, Dodd, Mead and Co.)

Wauchope, Robert (1962). *Lost Tribes and Sunken Continents. Myth and Method in the Study of American Indians.* Chicago, University of Chicago Press.

Wedel, Waldo R. (1957). "Observations on Some Nineteenth Century Pottery Vessels from the Upper Missouri," *Anthropological Papers* No. 51, Bulletin 164, Bureau of American Ethnology, Washington.

White, Leslie A. (ed.) (1942). "Lewis H. Morgan's Journal of a Trip to Southwestern Colorado and New Mexico, June 21 to August 7, 1878," *American Antiquity,* 8, pp. 1–26.

Willoughby, Charles C. (1905). "A Few Ethnological Specimens Collected by Lewis and Clarke," *American Anthropologist,* 7, pp. 633–41.

JOHN F. FREEMAN

The American Philosophical Society
in American Anthropology

THE American Philosophical Society for Promoting Useful Knowledge is the oldest learned society in this country, dating from 1743, and boasting such figures as Benjamin Franklin, David Rittenhouse, and Peter Stephen DuPonceau as early presidents. From the beginning a self-perpetuating body of distinguished scientists, scholars, and citizens, the Society within its first fifty years began collecting books and manuscripts for what has become a magnificent research library; and it initiated in 1769 the publication of its *Transactions*, a journal which continues together with a sister series to the present day. During the twentieth century the Society has also become a granting institution, furthering research in all disciplines, but it has given up its nineteenth century functions as advisor to the federal government on ethnological matters, as nascent anthropological society of Philadelphia, and, in the minds of a few, as Philadelphia's museum of anthropology. This discussion of the role of the American Philosophical Society in the history of American anthropology before 1900 will concentrate on these obsolete obligations.

As Whitfield J. Bell, Jr. (1962) has recently emphasized, the Society had, in the early years of this republic, something of a national character and certainly national pretensions. It enjoyed for a time an eminence not shared with its sister American Academy of Arts and Sciences at Boston (1780) or the American Antiquarian Society at Worcester (1812), for Philadelphia was the national capital until 1800, and Thomas Jefferson was simultaneously President of the

---

[1] The present paper is really a footnote to the excellent summary of A. Irving Hallowell (1960). See also Clark Wissler (1943), Franklin Edgerton (1944), and John C. Greene (1960). This paper is based principally on a two-year perusal of manuscript sources as well as on early publications; see John Finley Freeman (1961 and 1962).

Society and the nation. Bell has suggested that until 1846 the American Philosophical Society was de facto a National Academy of Sciences both as an honorific body and as the scientific organ of the federal government. For example, the Society's leading members gave expert advice to Meriwether Lewis before the departure of the Lewis and Clark Expedition, and special committees were appointed to advise the Long Expedition of 1819 and the Wilkes Expedition of 1838–1842 (Conklin, 1940).

The questions about land and Indians in the West which William Clark wrote down, apparently at Jefferson's dictation, clearly were a product of the combined efforts of Jefferson and members of the American Philosophical Society; and the use of a schedule of questions on ethnological and scientific subjects became standard, at the instance of the Society, for the later Long and Wilkes Expeditions. In fact it was this relationship which accounts for the reliance upon Jefferson's vocabulary list as late as 1877, when Powell published his *Introduction to the Study of Indian Languages*. While Jefferson's use of the question-and-answer approach to ethnology stems, I suspect, from the queries addressed to him by the Marquis de Marbois, queries which both occasioned and formed the outline of his *Notes on Virginia* (1787), his standard vocabulary list is derived in part from the list of the Empress Catherine. Jefferson had seen only the first volume of Pallas' work, undoubtedly the Latin version, for he tells Benjamin Smith Barton that "of the 250 words of my vocabularies and the 130 words of the great Russian vocabularies of the languages of the other quarters of the globe, 73 were common to both" (Jackson, 1962, pp. 465–66).[2] Since the second volume of Pallas includes an additional 155 words, a fair number of which are common to Jefferson's list, we must attribute these similarities to "independent invention" rather than to "diffusion." The printed version of Jefferson's vocabulary apparently dates from 1791 or early 1792, since the earliest surviving completed form (a Nanticoke vocabulary) was sent Jefferson in November 1792, while Jefferson took down his own vocabulary of the Poospatuck (Unquachog) on June 13, 1791, a list which is not similar to the printed form (Murray, 1792; Jefferson, 1791). We know that a bundle of these

[2] The reference is to Peter Simon Pallas (1786–1789), *Linguarun totius orbis vocabularia comparativa . . .* (St. Petersburg). The Russian version is dated 1787.

vocabulary forms was carried west by Lewis and Clark, that between nine and 23 forms were completed, and that a bundle of forms was among Lewis' effects in 1809 and presumably taken by Clark; but there the trail stops, although Nicholas Biddle in his notes of 1810 (?) mentions the vocabularies as if he had them in hand and later claims that they were turned over to Benjamin Smith Barton. These vocabularies have not yet been found, and Jefferson's cis-Mississippi collection was damaged by water in 1809.[3] While the whereabouts of the Lewis and Clark vocabularies may turn out to be of only antiquarian interest (as well it may, if the orthography of tribal names in the *journals* are any indication of their utility), what is important is that Jefferson gave the remains of his own collection to the new Historical and Literary Committee of the American Philosophical Society in 1818, and that Peter S. DuPonceau became Jefferson's heir in the study of American linguistics, beginning in 1820 his own collection of vocabularies copied from manuscript and printed sources.

DuPonceau transcribed not only the remains of Jefferson's collection, but also whatever other lists he could find, whether from manuscript or printed sources. He recognized the value of a uniform list (he had, in fact, urged Major Long to use the Jefferson form), and occasionally transposed existing lists to follow the Jefferson order. The vocabularies of trans-Mississippi Indians collected by Thomas Say on the Long expedition were copied from manuscript before Edwin James' report of the expedition was published, and most of the entries on that list correspond to Jefferson's (DuPonceau, 1820).[4]

---

[3] Jefferson's own memory is unreliable, as the many conflicting accounts written by him between 1809 and 1818 indicate. I rely on the inventory of Meriwether Lewis's effects printed in Jackson (1962, pp. 470–72); the references in Biddle's notes concerning the journals of Lewis and Clark, printed in Jackson (1962, pp. 499, 503, and 545); and Nicholas Biddle to William Tilghman, April 6, 1818, printed in Jackson (1962, pp. 635–37). The number of vocabularies taken is uncertain. The lower limit is the total instances mentioned in the journals; the upper is found in a memorandum of Clark, ca. January 1810, printed in Jackson (1962, p. 486).

[4] The book was begun in 1820 and is in the hand of both DuPonceau and his copyist, James R. Malenfant. The volume itself was consulted by Gallatin, while DuPonceau supplied copies of his copies to European correspondents. The indefatigable Albert S. Gatschet consulted this collection in 1888 (Gatschet, 1888).

The list used by Albert Gallatin for his comparative vocabulary of 53 Indian Languages in the *Synopsis* (1836) is derived from the Jefferson list. Gallatin had turned his attention to the American Indians about 1823 at the suggestion of Alexander von Humboldt (the *Synopsis* was a "sequel" to a paper written for Humboldt). In 1825–1826 he and Secretary of War James Barbour circulated a 600-word vocabulary to Indian agents and missionaries, but received only six replies, all of which are printed separately in the *Synopsis* (1836, pp. 381–404). The comparative vocabulary upon which Gallatin based his classifications uses a different 180-word list. Gallatin tells us (1836, pp. 1–2):

. . . every source of information, whether in manuscript or in works already published was resorted to. The selection of the words was necessarily controlled by the materials. Those and no others could be admitted, but such as were found in a number of the existing vocabularies, sufficient for the purpose intended. Some words of inferior importance were introduced only because they were common to almost all the vocabularies; and many have been omitted, because they were to be found only for a few dialects.[5]

That all but a dozen of the 180 words are from the Jefferson list is the result of Gallatin's relying principally upon DuPonceau's copy-book of vocabularies. Gallatin, long a member of the American Philosophical Society, naturally turned to that body for aid when his own vocabulary list failed to bring sufficient response, and DuPonceau generously lent his materials. With occasional additions to the various semantic categories, the Gallatin word list was used by Hale (Gallatin, 1848), Gibbs (1863), and by Powell (1877). The American Philosophical Society was thus the means by which a national standard word list for Indian languages was preserved and transmitted during the nineteenth century (Hallowell, 1960, p. 30; Gallatin, 1848; Gibbs, 1863; Powell, 1877).

Perhaps the first anthropological society in Philadelphia was the Standing Committee on Antiquities formed during the early years of Jefferson's presidency of the American Philosophical Society. Among its objectives were inquiry into "the Customs, Manners,

[5] The DuPonceau collection is collated with others in Gallatin (1848, pp. 305–67).

Languages, and Character of the Indian Nations," and the obtaining of descriptions "of ancient Fortifications, Tumuli, and other Indian works of Art," but no record remains of the committee's accomplishments. Since the committee did solicit, in a circular letter, specimens for the cabinet of the Society and communications for its *Transactions*, we can perhaps credit it with the several additions to the cabinet and with at least one of the seven articles in the *Transactions* between 1799 and 1809 which pertain to the American Indian (Turner, 1802).[6] (The others came through Benjamin Smith Barton, who was never a member of the Committee.) (Freeman, 1961, pp. 158–59; note 7, pp. 172–73.)

The successor to this early committee was the Historical and Literary Committee, founded in 1815, which had as its original purpose the collection of documents relating to the history and antiquities of the country. Peter S. DuPonceau, as secretary of the committee, pursued his linguistic researches in its name, carrying on for some years a correspondence with European philologists such as Vater, Klaproth, and Adelung, as well as with Americans such as Gallatin, John Pickering, and John Heckewelder. His researches were reflected in the first volume of *Transactions of the Historical and Literary Committee* (1819), in which were published DuPonceau's significant report on "the general character and forms of the languages of the American Indians," the correspondence of DuPonceau and Heckewelder upon the same subject, a Delaware vocabulary compiled by Heckewelder, and, of course, Heckewelder's famous "Account of the History, Manners, and Customs of the Indian Nations who once inhabited Pennsylvania and the Neighboring States." A careful examination of the manuscript correspondence between Heckewelder and DuPonceau shows DuPonceau not only as the skillful editor of Heckewelders *Account* but also as the originator of many of the ideas attributed to Heckewelder in the "Correspondence." DuPonceau saw to it that the volume was distributed to the appropriate people in America and Europe, and encouraged his brother, the Chevalier John DuPonceau, to translate the work into French. Heckewelder's international reputation was largely DuPonceau's doing but DuPonceau received European recognition when his study of Algonkian grammatical structure won the Vol-

---

[6] Judge Turner had himself donated the artifacts.

ney prize of the Institute de France in 1837 (Freeman, 1961, pp. 158–61).[7]

Despite the success of the *Transactions,* the American Philosophical Society itself was too impoverished, if not too uninterested, to continue to publish all the works DuPonceau projected for the committee, and, as irritated members drifted off to form the Historical Society of Pennsylvania (1824), DuPonceau was left with his vocabularies and his plans for publication. He became president of the American Philosophical Society in 1829, and during the next fifteen years managed to have the Society publish his translation and introduction to David Zeisberger's *Delaware Grammar* (DuPonceau, 1830), Heckewelder's study of Delaware Indian place names (1834), and Emanuel Naxera's Otomi grammar (1837). The last was a magnanimous gesture, since the Otomi was a major exception to DuPonceau's thesis that American Indian languages are all polysynthetic. DuPonceau's other linguistic studies are to be found in publications of the Massachusetts Historical Society and of the Historical Society of Pennsylvania, a second Historical and Literary Committee of the 1830s having taken a less active interest in American Indian materials.

The minutes of the Society and the various publications issued after DuPonceau's death suggest that the Society was a forum for anthropological discussion, but was never again in danger of becoming an anthropological society or of issuing a journal of anthropology. The *Transactions* included only six articles of anthropological interest between 1840 and 1900, a misleading fact, since the bulk of the anthropological papers read after 1838 appears in the *Proceedings* and since numbered among the six are Samuel G. Morton's sequel to his *Crania Americana* (1839), the *Crania Aegyptica* (1846), F. V. Hayden's huge study of the "Ethnography and Philology of the Indian Tribes of the Missouri Valley" (1862), and the striking reproduction of the "Tribute Roll of Montezuma" (Brinton, 1892).

[7] Copies of both outgoing and incoming letters were kept by DuPonceau in the "Letterbooks of the Historical and Literary Committee," now in the Library of the American Philosophical Society; Heckewelder's letters to DuPonceau are bound together in a single volume in that library, while Pickering's letters to DuPonceau are similarly bound in a volume in the Historical Society of Pennsylvania together with the bulk of DuPonceau's papers.

The *Proceedings* printed over one hundred communications pertaining to American anthropology between 1840 and 1900, nineteen of general interest, 33 relating to archaeology, and 54 on Indian linguistics. Before 1880, however, the relationship is quite different, for ten are of general interest, 23 are archaeological, and only eight concern linguistics. The shift in balance can be explained in terms of the subject and the persons offering papers.

The general papers before 1880 are brief and on a variety of subjects, generally amateur. The only modern-sounding ethnography is William More Gabb's study of Costa Rican tribes and languages (1875), a paper which antedated by twelve years Franz Boas' "Notes on the Ethnology of British Columbia" (1887), and these papers were exceptions to the rule. Even in 1897 J. Cheston Morris could address the Society on the relation to shamanism of a pentagonal dodecahedron found in 1792 and deposited in the Society's cabinets, and be supported in his speculations by Frank Hamilton Cushing. Most of the ethnographic work was published in linguistic papers, and there were no ethnographers other than Horatio Hale active in the Society.

The shift in balance between archaeology and linguistics reflects the influence of two men: Franklin Peale, who had published six archaeological papers by 1868, and Daniel G. Brinton, who published 28 linguistic papers after 1880. Peale, who was born in Philosophical Hall and named Benjamin Franklin by members of the Society, was a convinced monogenist. Excited by the concept of stone-age man, he began a collection of stone implements from American and European sites as convincing proof of the unity of mankind. His piety was unshaken by Boucher de Perthes, whom he dismissed as an enthusiast, for Peale refused to acknowledge the great antiquity of man (extinct animals, he argued, had become extinct later than supposed). Upon his death, his collection of 1800 artifacts, "implements of the Stone Age . . . collected and arranged as impressively confirming the unity of the human race," was willed to the American Philosophical Society, apparently as footnotes to his articles. The paleontologist, Edward Drinker Cope, who published frequently in the *Proceedings* during the last decades of the nineteenth century, took the other side of the question, not only admitting the antiquity of man in Europe, but also arguing for similar interpretations of American sites. In 1893 he noted with delight the absurd assumption of the "Washington people," W. H. Holmes and the Bureau of Ethnology personnel, that flaked stone points found near the Potomac were only objects from the making of polished points, when none of the latter had been seen at the site (Cope, 1893).[8]

Brinton dominated anthropological publication in the *Proceedings*, not only in terms of the volume of his own writing, but also in that he introduced and recommended or disapproved the publication of papers by nonmembers. The bulk of his papers concern Latin American languages, especially vocabularies, classification, and translations of specific terms in order to trace the spread of certain concepts in Middle America. The Latin American papers are based principally upon historical documents and manuscript materials, and only infrequently upon material supplied Brinton by his contemporaries. [It is worth noting that Brinton's early studies of the Muskogee (1870) and the Natchez (1873) made use of native informants.] The most interesting of his linguistic papers are his respectful summary of Wilhelm von Humboldt's philosophy of language (1885a), his favorable assessment of DuPonceau's belief that all American Indian languages are polysynthetic (1885b), his engaging analysis of terms for "love" in various American languages (1885c), and his speculative but positive description of what the language of paleolithic man must have been like (a mixture, as I understand it, of basic noises to indicate a person and a confusion of "alternating sounds"). (Brinton, 1888; American Philosophical Society, *Classified Index*, 1940).

Omitting Brinton's articles still leaves important contributions in linguistics. In 1846 Samuel Stehman Haldeman reported that on the basis of his field experience the phonology of the Wyandot was not impossible to record. In 1868 F. V. Hayden published Pawnee and Winnebago paradigms and vocabularies, and over a fifteen-year period Albert S. Gatschet wrote on the Tonkawa (1876a), Timucua (1876b, 1878, 1880), Aruba (1885a) and Beothuk (1885b, 1886,

[8] For a complete listing of papers published, see *Classified Index*, (1940). The Peale papers are printed in the *Proceedings* of the American Philosophical Society, 1860, (7, pp. 411–16), 1861 (8, pp. 265–72), 1864 (9, pp. 401–3, 460), 1868 (10, pp. 243–44, 430–35).

1890), and published texts from the Isleta Tewa (1891). In 1883 Horatio Hale announced that the Tutelo were Siouan speakers. In 1885 and 1886, W. J. Hoffman published vocabularies of the Yokuts and Salish (Flathead), while in 1891 Franz Boas published the vocabularies of the Tlingit, Haida, and Tsimshian (1891) which Horatio Hale would not let him include in the reports to the British Association for the Advancement of Science. This was followed by his Kwakiutl vocabulary (1893) and Bella Coola texts (1895), which together with the Passamaquoddy texts published by J. Dyneley Prince in 1897 and 1899 suggested a new era of linguistic studies.

The American Philosophical Society did not become an anthropological museum. Although in the early years of the nineteenth century Peale's museum had been housed in Philosophical Hall, the Society had obviously borne in mind the distinction between a museum as a catch-all of curios to amuse the public and a cabinet as a reference tool for students of natural history and geology. A few Indian artifacts had come into the Society's cabinet in the 1790s, but the cabinet remained small until the gifts of Peruvian and Mexican materials made by Joel R. Poinsett in 1820 and 1830. This collection, together with specimens donated at the same time by William H. Keating, amounted to some 2,800 items. The Poinsett-Keating collection was internationally famous, mentioned in European journals, and studied by artists and archaeologists during succeeding years (American Philosophical Society, *Transaction*, 1830, pp. 510–11).[9]

As the cabinets for the various sciences grew, a shortage of space developed. Similar difficulties faced the Academy of Natural Sciences in Philadelphia, for its collections had not only grown enormously, but had also developed in fields inappropriate to an institution devoted to natural science and natural history. Early in 1864 the Academy passed a resolution suggesting that the American Philosophical Society receive on deposit the Academy's archaeological specimens, with the Society reciprocating by depositing its natural history specimens at the Academy, in order to make of the Academy *the* Philadelphia museum for natural history and the sciences, and of the Philosophical *the* museum for archaeology, antiquities,

[9] Several lists of the contents of the collection are to be found in the curator's records in the archives of the Society.

"and human improvements." Franklin Peale greeted the suggestion enthusiastically and moved that the American Philosophical Society transfer its natural history specimens to the Academy of Natural Sciences (American Philosophical Society, *Proceedings*, 1864). When Peale's widow died in 1875, her attorney informed the Society that it was to receive the Peale Stone Age Collection (*Proceedings*, 1875), provided that the collection be preserved in fireproof quarters and that the collection, as arranged by Peale, be open to the inspection of the public. The Society accepted, but lacking a fireproof building it allowed the collection to remain in the vault of the Philadelphia Savings Fund until 1877, when Robert Patterson, the Peale executor, respectfully suggested that the collection be deposited in the Academy of Natural Sciences, which had only recently completed a fireproof wing to its building (*Proceedings*, 1877a). The Society agreed, voting to deposit the Poinsett-Keating collection in that museum as well (*ibid.*, 1877b). In 1880, when the Society received some 10,000 "arrowheads" collected by the late Samuel Stehman Haldeman, this collection also went over to the Academy. And there the artifacts rested until 1891 (*ibid.*, 1880).

Extensive alterations to Philosophical Hall were undertaken during the summer of 1890, when a third story was added for the growing library, and the four rooms on the second floor were made into two. The entire building was fireproofed (*ibid.*, 1890). A year later a resolution was passed asking the return of the Peale collection in accordance with the terms of Mrs. Peale's will (*ibid.*, 1891), and early in 1892 the collection was back in Philosophical Hall (*ibid.*, 1892a). Within a month a resolution was passed (*ibid.*, 1892b), urging the return of all specimens at the Academy, the Historical Society of Pennsylvania, and the Numismatic and Antiquarian Society. Two reports from the curators of the Philosophical Society during the remainder of 1892 (*ibid.*, 1892c, 1892d) showed a division of opinion: only J. Cheston Morris wanted to make a museum of the North Room (upstairs) and to make the Poinsett-Keating collection the stellar attraction.

An additional complication was presented when Sara Y. Stevenson wrote suggesting that the new University Museum was surely the most sensible home for the Poinsett-Keating collection, for here it could be studied as part of a series, not in isolation. The matter

came to a head in February, when the motion to withdraw the
Poinsett-Keating collection from the Academy was presented (*ibid.,*
1893b). Morris was for the move, Daniel G. Brinton and the majority were against. The minutes tell us "an animated debate ensued...,"
and with the subsequent vote the Society gave up its archaeological museum (*ibid.,* 1893c). By the end of April, the chairman of the
Hall Committee had unceremoniously dumped many of Morris' museum specimens out on the floor, damaging some plaster casts and
mixing up the labels *(ibid.,* 1893a). By 1900 the Peale collection had
been returned to the Academy of Natural Sciences, where all the
anthropological collections of the American Philosophical Society
remained until 1933 and 1937, when they were transferred to the
University Museum, where they are housed to this day.

Had the Society made an anthropological museum of its quarters,
it might have been spared a threat to its existence in 1899. From the
days of Charles Willson Peale on, it had been customary for the
Society to rent out part of its building to various tenants, including
artist Thomas Sully, the Athenaeum, and the City of Philadelphia.
In 1891 the first floor was let to a stock brokerage (*Philadelphia
Telegram,* 1891) and in 1899 the Historical Society of Pennsylvania,
the Colonial Society of Pennsylvania (*Philadelphia Bulletin,* 1899)
and the Pennsylvania Society of the Sons of the Revolution urged
the City Council to purchase Philosophical Hall and tear it down:
commercialism in Independence Square was sacrilege. It is fortunate
that the plot did not succeed, for during the twentieth century the
American Philosophical Society has gone on to sponsor anthropological research and publication while its library's collection of Indian manuscript materials and tapes has become a research center
for anthropology, and its archives house the history of early American anthropology.

REFERENCES

American Philosophical Society (1940). *Classified Index to the Publications of the American Philosophical Society.* Philadelphia.
———(1836). Letter to Mahlon Dickerson. (In MS archives of A.P.S.)

American Philosophical Society, *Proceedings* (1864). Minutes, March 18, Vol. 9, pp. 353–54.

——(1875). Minutes, November 5, Vol. 14, pp. 646–50.

——(1877a). Minutes, October 5, Vol. 17, pp. 13–15.

——(1877b). Minutes, November 16, Vol. 17, p. 273.

——(1880). Minutes, December 3, Vol. 20, p. 194.

——(1890). Minutes, April 16, Vol. 28, pp. 101, 248.

——(1891). Minutes, December 4, Vol. 29, p. 165.

——(1892a). Minutes, February 19, Vol. 30, p. 11.

——(1892b). Minutes, March 18, Vol. 30, p. 122.

——(1892c). Minutes, May 6, Vol. 30, p. 262.

——(1892d). Minutes, December 16, Vol. 30, p. 316.

——(1893a). Curator's report, (M.S. in curator's records in archives of A.P.S.)

——(1893b). Minutes, February 3, Vol. 31, p. 13.

——(1893c). Minutes, February 10, Vol. 31, p. 133.

American Philosophical Society, *Transactions* (1830), N.S. 3, pp. 503, 510, 511.

Bell, Whitfield J., Jr. (1962). "The American Philosophical Society as a National Academy of Sciences," paper read before the Tenth International Congress of the History of Science, Philadelphia, September 1, 1962.

Boas, Franz (1887). "Notes on the Ethnology of British Columbia," A.P.S., *Proceedings*, 24, pp. 422–28.

——(1891). "Vocabularies of the Tlingit, Haida, and Tsimshian Languages," A.P.S., *Proceedings*, 29, pp. 173–208.

——(1893). "Vocabulary of the Kwakiutl Language," A.P.S., *Proceedings*, 31, pp. 34–82.

——(1895), "Salishan Texts," A.P.S., *Proceedings*, 34, pp. 31–48.

Brinton, Daniel G. (1870). "Contributions to a Grammar of the Muskokee Language," A.P.S., *Proceedings*, 11, pp. 301–9.

——(1873). "Language of the Natchez," A.P.S., *Proceedings*, 13, pp. 483–99.

——(1885a), "The Philosophic Grammar of American Language, as Set Forth by Wilhelm von Humboldt," A.P.S., *Proceedings*, 23, pp. 306–31.

——(1885b). "Polysynthesis and Incorporation as Characteristics of American Languages," A.P.S., *Proceedings*, 23, pp. 48–86.

——(1885c). "The Conception of Love in Some American Languages," A.P.S., *Proceedings*, 23, pp. 546–61.

———(1888). "The Language of Palaeolithic Man," A.P.S., *Proceedings,* 25, pp. 212–25.

———(1893). "A Vocabulary of the Nanticoke Dialect," A.P.S., *Proceedings,* 31, pp. 325–33.

Brinton, Daniel G. (with Henry Phillips Jr. and J. Cheston Morris) (1892). "The Tribute Roll of Montezuma," A.P.S., *Transactions,* 17, pp. 53–61.

Conklin, Edwin G. (1940). "Connection of the American Philosophical Society with our First National Exploring Expedition," A.P.S., *Proceedings,* 82, pp. 519–41.

Cope, E. D. (1893). "Stone Implements from Maryland, on the Patomac," A.P.S., *Proceedings,* 31, pp. 229–31.

Dickerson, Mahlon (U.S. Navy Department) (1836a). Letter to Peter S. DuPonceau, August 31, 1836. (In manuscript archives of A.P.S.)

———(1836b). Letter to Peter S. DuPonceau, November 19, 1836. (*Ibid.*)

DuPonceau, Peter S. (1820). *Indian Vocabularies.* . . . (Copybook in the library of the A.P.S.)

———(1830). "Grammar of the Language of the Lenni Lenape, or Delaware Indians. Translated from the German MS. of the Late Rev. D. Zeisberger," A.P.S., *Transactions,* N.S. 3, pp. 65–251.

DuPonceau, Peter S. (with Samuel Brown, R. M. Patterson, and Robert Walsh) (1819?). "Concerning Inquiries to be Made by Major Long of the Indians [ca. 30 March, 1819]." MS. Communications to the A.P.S., *Philosophy, Literature and Language,* 2 (1819). (In MS. archives of A.P.S.)

Edgerton, Franklin (1944). "Notes on Early American Work in Linguistics," A.P.S., *Proceedings,* 87, pp. 25–34.

Freeman, John Finley (1961). "The American Indian in Manuscript: Preparing a Guide to Holdings in the Library of the American Philosophical Society," *Ethnohistory,* 8, pp. 156–78.

———(1962). "Manuscript Sources on Latin American Indians in the Library of the American Philosophical Society," A.P.S., *Proceedings,* 106, pp. 530–40.

Gabb, William More (1875). "Indian Tribes and Languages of Costa Rica," A.P.S., *Proceedings,* 14, pp. 483–602.

Gallatin, Albert (1836). "A Synopsis of the Indian Tribes within the United States East of the Rocky Mountains and in the British and Russian Possessions in North America," *Archaeologica Americana: Transactions and Collections of the American Antiquarian Society.*

———(1848). "Hale's Indians of North-West America, and Vocabularies of North America," American Ethnological Society, *Transactions,* 2.

Gatschet, Albert S. (1876a). "Remarks upon the Tonkawa Language," A.P.S., *Proceedings,* 16, pp. 318–27.

———(1876b). "The Timucua Language," *ibid.,* 16, pp. 626–42.

———(1878). "The Timucua Language," *ibid.,* 17, pp. 490–504.

———(1880). "The Timucua Language," *ibid.,* 18, pp. 465–502.

———(1885a). "The Aruba Language and the Papiamento Jamgon," *ibid.,* 22, pp. 299–305.

———(1885b). "The Beothuk Indians," *ibid.,* 22, pp. 408–24.

———(1886). "The Beothuk Indians," *ibid.,* 23, pp. 411–33.

———(1888). Letter to Henry Phillips, October 29, 1888. (In library of A.P.S.)

———(1890). "The Beothuk Indians," A.P.S., *Proceedings,* 28, pp. 1–16.

———(1891). "A Mythic Tale of the Isleta Indians," *ibid.,* 29, pp. 208–18.

Gibbs, George (1863). "Instructions for Research Relative to Ethnology and Philology of America," *Smithsonian Miscellaneous Collection,* No. 160. Washington, D.C.

Greene, John C. (1960). "Early Scientific Interest in the American Indian: Comparative Linguistics," A.P.S., *Proceedings,* 104, pp. 511–17.

Haldeman, Samuel Steman (1846). "Remarks on the Phonology of the Wyandots," *ibid.,* 4, pp. 268–69.

Hale, Horatio (1883). "The Tutelo Tribe and Language," *ibid.,* 21, pp. 1–47.

Hallowell, A. Irving (1960). "The Beginnings of Anthropology in America," in Frederica de Laguna (ed.), *Selected Papers from the American Anthropologist, 1888–1920,* pp. 1–90. Evanston, Ill.

Hayden, F. V. (1862). "Ethnography and Philology of the Indian Tribes of the Missouri Valley," A.P.S., *Transactions,* 12, pp. 231–461.

———(1868). "Brief Notes on the Pawnee, Winnebago and Omaha Languages," A.P.S., *Proceedings,* 10, pp. 389–421.

Heckewelder, John (1834). "Names Which the Lenni Lenape or Delaware Indians . . . Had Given to Rivers, Streams, Places, etc. . . ," A.P.S., *Transactions,* N.S. 4, pp. 351–96.

Hoffman, W. J. (1885). "Vocabulary of the Selish Language," A.P.S., *Proceedings,* 23, pp. 361–71.

———(1886). "Vocabulary of the Waitshum'ni Dialect of the Kawi'a Language," *ibid.,* 24, pp. 372–79.

Jackson, Donald (ed.) (1962). *Letters of the Lewis and Clark Expedition.* Urbana, Ill.

Jefferson, Thomas (1791). "Vocabulary of the Unquachog" (In MS archives of A.P.S.)

46   JOHN F. FREEMAN

Morris, J. Cheston (1897). "Relation of the Pentagonal Dodecahedron Found Near Marietta, Ohio, to Shamanism" (includes comments by Cushing), A.P.S., *Proceedings*, 36, pp. 179–92.

Morton, Samuel G. (1846). "Observations on Egyptian Ethnography," A.P.S., *Transactions*, 9, pp. 93–159.

Murray, William Vans (1792). Letter to Thomas Jefferson, September 18, 1792, printed in D.G. Brinton, (1893), "Vocabulary of the Nanticoke," (in MS archives, A.P.S.)

Naxera, Emmanuele (1837). "De Lingua Othomitorum Dissertatio," A.P.S., *Transactions*, N.S. 5, pp. 249–96.

Philadelphia Bulletin (1899). November 27, 1899. (News clipping in curator's record in archives of A.P.S.)

Philadelphia Telegram (1891). July 20, 1891. (News clipping in curator's record in archives of A.P.S.)

Powell, J. W. (1877). Introduction to the Study of Indian Languages, with Works, Phrases, and Sentences to be Collected. Washington. (2nd edition, 1880.)

Prince, S. Dyneley (1897). "The Passamaquoddy Wampum Records," A.P.S., *Proceedings*, 36, pp. 479–95.

———(1899). "Some Passamaquoddy Witchcraft Tales," A.P.S., *Proceedings*, 38, pp. 181–89.

Turner, George (1802). "Remarks on Certain Articles Found in an Indian Tumulus at Cincinnati and Now Deposited in the Museum of the American Philosophical Society," A.P.S., *Transactions*, O.S. 5, pp. 74–75.

Wissler, Clark (1943). "The American Indian and the American Philosophical Society," A.P.S., *Proceedings*, 86, pp. 189–204.

HARRY L. SHAPIRO

The Direction of
Physical Anthropology

IT IS now over 125 years ago that Dr. Samuel G. Morton of this city published his massive *Crania Americana*, an opus that achieved an international reputation for him and that in retrospect won him recognition as the "father" of physical anthropology in the United States. One could scarcely select a more appropriate combination of a man and his work to symbolize the origins of the emergent physical anthropology of the time.

The practice customary in this country of linking physical anthropology with archaeology, ethnology, and linguistics to form the broad discipline of anthropology has obscured the fact that physical anthropology also has roots in anatomy and biology that are quite independent of its intellectual and historical connections with anthropology. Because it shared, however, with ethnology and archaeology an interest in the origin and development of the peoples of the earth, it came to be associated closely with them, but its beginnings were an outgrowth of systematic zoology, its methods were borrowed from comparative anatomy, and its practitioners were drawn from among those trained in the study of the human organism. Blumenbach, Camper, Broca, Virchow, to name only a few of the early pioneers, were anatomists and physicians first before they became physical anthropologists. Morton, as the first great name in American physical anthropology, was equally well suited by profession to deal with the raw data of the subject. He had been trained in medicine and had been appointed professor of anatomy in the Pennsylvania Medical College in 1839, the year of the publication of his master work. With this background and training he was following a tradition well established among his European contemporaries in this field that was just becoming identified as physical anthropology.

The *Crania Americana*, although scarcely read nowadays, is often considered a pioneer work. In a sense it is, but its inspiration I believe comes from a concern that was far from being as novel as this would imply. Back of Morton lay 300 years of interest and speculation in the nature and origin of the peoples of the New World. The Spaniards had hardly begun their conquests before they started to form competing systems to explain the astonishing fact that a whole branch of mankind was seated in the new-found world with no apparent connections with the rest of the known universe of man. Oviedo and Acosta, writing in the generation immediately after Columbus, explored various explanations. Oviedo favored a connection with the Canaanites driven out by the Israelites. Acosta sought a number of possible migration routes from Europe and was, even as early as this, already refuting the origin of the Indians from the Lost Tribes of Israel. It was this discovery of a new variety of man, later reinforced by similar encounters with other previously unknown races, that came as a fundamental enlargement of the European view of man, and more than any other one fact stimulated the extension of an already active systematic zoology into the realm of *Homo sapiens*, thus laying the foundations of physical anthropology.

Although this preoccupation with the general problem of human classification into races and varieties on the basis of physical characteristics formed the substance of physical anthropology, in the New World, and in the United States in particular, the specific problem of the American Indian, his relationship to other groups of men, and his origins, was not lost in the more general problem of the differentiation of the species. It continued to be discussed and debated until virtually every possible notion had been proposed by one writer or another. Nor was it restricted only to a narrow group of scholars and investigators. Jefferson reflected on several occasions the widespread interest in the subject which had come to permeate a wide range of general literature and reference. Thus Morton, in applying the newly developed descriptive and comparative techniques of dealing with the anatomical remains of the American Indian, was attacking a very old problem. In his zeal he amassed for his time a very extensive and important collection of crania that later was deposited in the Academy of Natural Sciences in Philadelphia. This, together with the cranial collections at the Wistar, gave Philadelphia in these early days a distinct pre-eminence as a center for the study of the varieties of man. This reputation was further enhanced by such successors of Morton as Meigs, Leidy, and Gliddon, all from Philadelphia and all following the same line of inquiry and interest. In Boston, too, Wyman and Warren were pursuing similar studies, thereby contributing to the establishment of physical anthropology as a branch of science with its characteristic method and its definitive area of research.

Although these formative years, here and abroad, established the physical differentiation of man into races and varieties as the perennial problem of physical anthropology, this was not to remain the sole or, in its narrow sense, the dominant concern of the contemporary descendants of Morton. The present diversification of interests that characterizes physical anthropology—ranging from anatomy to genes and from fossils to blood groups—came about in a number of ways.

There was, to begin with, an inevitable expansion of subject matter as the initial exploration led investigators into the development of techniques, methods, and comparative studies dealing with related organisms. The phenomenon of variation itself, often distinct from its classification into zoological categories, emerged as a valid interest worthy of study for itself.

Twenty years after Morton's *Crania Americana* appeared, Darwin published the *Origin of Species*, which was eventually to have a profound effect not only on biology in general but upon physical anthropology in particular. The fossils relating to man's evolution that had been uncovered before this time had not been valued or understood, since there was no intellectual frame in which they could be placed. The Gibraltar skull, for example, was virtually forgotten, although disinterred only a decade before Darwin. Even the Neanderthal skull, discovered in 1856 and dismissed as merely a pathological *Homo sapiens* by Virchow, found a proper niche for itself only after the new theory of the evolution of man provided one for it. How many precious fossils have been irretrievably lost to us because they were uncovered prematurely no one can ever know.

The doctrine of the biological evolution of man found a congenial reception on the whole from anthropology, since, among all the recognized disciplines in the intellectual and scientific life of Western Europe and America, it was by the nature of its dedication to the study of the development of culture conditioned both to a generous time perspective and to a recognition of the process of change and evolution. For physical anthropology, evolution opened a vast new vista of time and dynamic change. It enhanced the value of its comparative studies of the primates, and gave a new interest to its continuing study of human races. As the fossil relics of man's ancestors came to light, they fell to physical anthropology, which was the discipline most suited by virtue of its established interests and techniques to deal with them. But by the very nature of the problem they presented they also served to maintain the links of physical anthropology with anatomy and zoology.

This easy absorption of a new field by virtue of its methodological competence is also illustrated in another expansion of the area covered by physical anthropology. Although Quetelet in Belgium had concerned himself with the quantitative and mathematical study of stature, it was Bowditch in this country who stimulated the study of the quantitative growth patterns of children in association with socioeconomic conditions. The anthropometric methods already developed by physical anthropology for recording in precise terms the quantitative variations of the human body enabled it to participate effectively in the subsequent exploitation of this new field of research, which came to embrace a broad segment of growth and development.

If in its own growth and development physical anthropology invaded and pre-empted new fields of inquiry with its peculiar methods and for its own purposes, it was also stimulated to expansion by the advances in various biological sciences that offered new methodologies and procedures by which to explore its traditional themes. Genetics is one example, and immunology another. Even early in the formative years of physical anthropology, Broca had written on hybridism in man. This was a subject that would perhaps inevitably have arisen in a discipline concerned at the time primarily with racial classification. But Broca like many another was premature and was unable to make any truly significant contribution. It is of more than passing interest that only a few years after 1900, the effective date for the modern development of genetics, it was

Farrabee, an American anthropologist, subsequently on the staff of the University Museum in Philadelphia, who made the first application of Mendelian genetics to the study of heredity in man. His investigation of the inheritance of brachydactyly was a landmark, and he was soon followed by Eugen Fischer, who examined with the new analytical tools of genetics a racially mixed population—the Rehobother Bastards of South Africa.

The serological groups—the ABO blood types—discovered by Landsteiner in 1900 illustrate another borrowing to the enrichment of present-day physical anthropology. The observation of the Hirszfelds that the various national groups imprisoned in Turkey during World War I yielded significantly different blood type distributions was epochal. Immediately after peace was restored it let loose a veritable flood of reports on the blood group distributions of virtually every major group of mankind. Physical anthropologists, recognizing the potential value of these data to racial problems, participated actively with geneticists and others in the collection and exploitation of such information. The series of inquiries begun in those days has led to further serological discoveries. And the end is not yet in this active and promising field.

By this multifold process of exploring the ramification of its original problem and developing appropriate methods, by moving into new fields of cognate interest because of the possession of suitable techniques, and by borrowing from the discoveries of still other sciences, physical anthropology has undergone a notable growth. The cliché of the physical anthropologist with calipers in hand recording cephalic indices has long been out of date. A glance at the content of the journals of this specialty over the past generation quickly reveals that the preoccupation of the physical anthropologists has grown and diversified with the development of the biological sophistication of the sciences related to it. Indeed the content of research in this area has become at present so diverse, calling on so many specialties and requiring such a multiplicity of skills, that there is already evident a marked tendency toward a division of labor and interest. For physical anthropology comes closest of any recognized branch of the biological sciences toward fulfilling the requirements of a human biology. To discuss, therefore, the present problems of this branch of anthropology in a limited space of time is a hopeless task. I have, therefore, presented this brief historical sketch of physical anthropology not so much as a preface to a discussion of its current activities, which are probably fairly well known to most of you, but to point out a direction which I think its future may take.

It is indeed curious that in spite of at least 150 years of exposure to the concept of culture as elaborated by its sister sciences in anthropology, physical anthropology itself has remained remarkably unaffected by it. It is true, of course, that chronological frames of reference based on culture dynamics have been a part of physical anthropology, and in other incidental ways as well culture has not been entirely ignored. But this is a secondary use of the concept and not a primary application to the very heart of the subject matter with which it is concerned. In fact, as I have already indicated, the trend of physical anthropology over the past 75 years or more has been toward an increasing involvement with general biological developments. And in recent years this has reached the point where it has often, privately at least, been discussed whether traditional associations of physical anthropology are meaningful or helpful any longer.

And yet as a few of us are now coming to see with increasing conviction, culture must be examined as a basic factor in human biology and as a determinant of the direction of human evolution. Although we sometimes generalize about culture as an expression of the biological nature of man and do little more with it than that, it is equally true that man in many ways is deeply affected in his biological expressions by the culture that surrounds him. This interplay of culture and human biology began to take on specific meaning as the result of at least a couple of recent conceptualizations of the evolutionary process.

One of these comes from the insight into the adaptive process that geneticists, paleontologists, zoologists, and others have recently sharpened and focused. From the laboratory and field studies of these specialities, it seems clear that the gene pool of a breeding population is the continuum of which individual organisms are merely ephemeral expressions, varying according to the genetic potentialities of each genotype interacting with the environment, and that the gene pool changes in time according to the differential reproductive rates of its various members. These differences in reproduction reflect in the long run the selective effect of the physical environment. Thus, over time the population comes to take on an increasing integration with the environment, which we call adaptation. Moreover, the process is such that the adaptations of a species or a variety may define the very ecological niche to which it has become adapted, an entity that otherwise is not always readily recognizable.

At the same time, the most recent investigations into the fossil history of man had brought into relief the possibility that the beginning of human technology as it survives in the simplest form of pebble tools, associated now with primitive hominids, is one of the turning points in the emergence of a man-like creature distinguishable from all other primates. It is technology that forms the beginning of that most human of all achievements—culture. Even with its first appearance it altered fundamentally man's environment. And as it has evolved and mediated more and more the physical environment in which man lives, it must have assumed a greater role in the selective process itself. Similarly, language and social organization form a part of the culture which early man developed and by which he was influenced. After a million years more or less, it is obvious man has become a creature adapted to culture, that he can no longer survive in anything like his present state without it. He has created the very ecological niche to which he has become adapted. Moreover, the fact that the cultural environment is one that has undergone remarkable changes in a relatively short time provides a clue to the notable speed of human evolution in brain size, the area of the human organism most sensitive to the demands of culture.

If there could be any doubt that man's evolution and his culture are mutually dependent, the situation in which man finds himself today must dispel the illusion. Nothing in the immediate future of physical anthropology offers a greater challenge than the exploration and understanding of this interacting relationship. And for those of us who see an inevitability in the increasing need that man will face in the future of taking a more conscious part in directing his own evolution, this development is an essential one.

The role of culture in determining the biological characteristics of man offers more opportunities for investigation as well. What effect, for example, do various types of social and cultural organization and differentiation exert in maintaining genetic isolates? Does language, which must by anthropological definition be regarded as an expression of culture, exert a selective pressure upon the early evolution of man and later act in inhibiting or encouraging gene flow? What are the consequences of urbanization, population density, and other cultural developments on the immunological resources, growth patterns, and other biological phenomena of man? These and many other queries of the same order suggest themselves. One can dare predict that as inquiry in this promising direction continues and becomes increasingly sophisticated, it will uncover relationships we can now scarcely formulate. If physical anthropology had not already by the accident of its birth and early development acquired a close relationship with the branches of anthropology that are concerned with culture, it would now have to seek it in the interests of its fullest development.

H. M. WORMINGTON

The Paleo-Indian

IT IS truly amazing how many major contributions to our knowledge of the Paleo-Indian stage in North America have been made by individuals and institutions in the Philadelphia area. Without these contributions we should know far less about the early inhabitants of this continent. Although there are still many gaps in our knowledge, it is remarkable that we have as much information as we do, for only forty years have elapsed since it was definitely established that man had entered the New World during the Pleistocene.

The 1926 discovery, near Folsom, New Mexico, of a projectile point in unmistakable association with the bones of an extinct species of bison marked the beginning of a whole new field of archaeological research (Cook, 1927; Figgins, 1927). In the intervening years we have learned more about these early bison hunters who made fluted points that are examples of truly great flint work. Investigations at the Lindenmeier Folsom site in Colorado, where John L. Cotter and Loren Eiseley participated in the excavations, have provided knowledge of the tools, other than projectile points, that were used by the Folsom people (Roberts, 1935, 1936). Radiocarbon dates from this site and from a locality near Lubbock, Texas have shown that Folsom man roamed the Western United States between 8000 and 9000 B.C. (Haynes and Agogino, 1960).

Further studies in the Plains area have shown that there were still earlier occupations, that there were hunters with a different tradition who were contemporaneous with Folsom, and that there is a whole series of complexes that are post-Folsom in age, but still of considerable antiquity.

Not until 1932 was evidence found that Paleo-Indians had hunted elephants as well as extinct bison. In that year, at the site near Dent, Colorado, two large fluted points, of the type now called Clovis, were found with bones of Columbian mammoth (Figgins, 1933). A recent radiocarbon date obtained from the bone is 11,200 ± 500 years ago, or 9250 B.C. (Agogino, personal communication).

Clovis points have since been found in association with mammoth in a number of localities in the Western United States, but the most important site is the one that gave the name to this type. This is the Blackwater Draw locality near Clovis, New Mexico, first excavated by the late Edgar B. Howard and John L. Cotter on behalf of the Academy of Natural Sciences of Philadelphia and the University of Pennsylvania Museum (Howard, 1935a and 1935b; Cotter, 1937, 1938). This site yielded not only Clovis points but some extremely interesting bone tools, and it provided stratigraphic evidence that Clovis preceded Folsom, and that Folsom points in turn were older than the beautifully flaked unfluted lanceolate points found in the area.

Edgar Howard's contributions to the Early Man field can scarcely be overestimated. Not only did he undertake important excavations and publish significant reports, but he was responsible for the International Symposium on Early Man, held in the Philadelphia Academy of Natural Sciences in 1937. This meeting, which brought together distinguished scholars from all parts of the world, was one of the real milestones in the study of Early Man. Dr. Howard also played a leading role in organizing a conference on terminology, held in Santa Fe in 1941, which did a great deal to clarify problems relating to the catch-all category called "Yuma."

Since then much information has been gained about the various complexes of hunters of Pleistocene bison who used the finely flaked unfluted projectile points which were once grouped under the term Yuma. Loren Eiseley was among the first to focus attention on the important Scottsbluff type of projectile point (Schultz and Eiseley, 1935, 1936). Of tremendous significance was the definition of the Cody Complex, of which this is a part. It was Linton Satterthwaite and the late Dr. Howard who excavated the Finley site in the Eden Valley of Wyoming (Howard, Satterthwaite, and Bache, 1941; Satterthwaite, 1957). Valuable reports on the geology were also published by the University Museum (Moss, 1951). Finely flaked points of the type that now bears the name Eden had been found in blowouts, but it was at the Finley site that they were first found in situ and that it was determined that they and Scottsbluff points were part of the same complex.

Further important data were obtained at the Horner site near Cody, Wyoming, excavated by Glenn L. Jepsen of Princeton University (Jepsen, 1951, 1953). Here were found not only magnificent examples of Scottsbluff and Eden points in association with bison remains, but also a number of other tools, including asymmetrically stemmed cutting implements now known as Cody knives. A Princeton geologist, Sheldon Judson, helped to date this complex, which appears to have an age of the general magnitude of 5000 to 7000 B.C. Radiocarbon dates of 8750 ± 120 years (6800 B.C.) and 8840 (6890 B.C.) have been obtained from samples from this site. (Science, 144, 326).

It is a protégé of J. Alden Mason, George Agogino, who has done a great deal to clarify the sequence of early complexes in the Northern Plains and to obtain dates. The American Philosophical Society has provided grants for some of this work. He has defined a new point type, a lanceolate, slightly stemmed form, called the Hell Gap type, and obtained a radiocarbon date from an horizon in the type station in Wyoming that contains such specimens (Agogino, 1961). The date of 8890 B.C. indicates that there were other hunters who used a different type of weapon tip who were contemporaries of the makers of Folsom points. At the Hell Gap site Agate Basin points, which have a somewhat similar form but which are unstemmed, and Cody points, have been found in two sequent levels overlying the Hell Gap horizon. Radiocarbon dates for the Agate Basin horizon at another site ranged between 7400 and 8040 B.C. (Agogino and Frankforter, 1960).[1]

It was Froelich Rainey who first reported the discovery of an Agate Basin point, although the type did not then bear that name (Rainey, 1940). It lay frozen in situ sixty feet below the surface at

[1] Intensive excavation of this complex site has shown that the edge of the creek bed where the radiocarbon sample was obtained, three cultural horizons, which are separate in other parts of the site, had merged into a single artifact-bearing horizon. It now appears that the Hell Gap type is of somewhat more recent age than was originally thought, and that the horizon in which it occurs postdates that which has produced Agate Basin points. The Cody horizon which lies above the Agate Basin levels has produced a radiocarbon date of 6640 B.C. ± 600 years (H. Irwin, C. Irwin-Williams, G. Agogino, personal communication).

Ester Creek, Alaska, in association with a mastodon bone. Other Arctic finds will not be discussed here, since this subject has been presented by Chester Chard in a subsequent paper, but it should be noted that it was Dr. Rainey who found the first evidence of a core and blade industry in Alaska, and that it was J. L. Giddings, Jr., representing the University of Pennsylvania, who discovered the extremely important Denbigh Flint Complex at Norton Sound (Giddings, 1951).

In the Eastern United States, in the area that stretches from the Great Plains to the Atlantic Seaboard, have been found a great many Clovis points and other large fluted points. They have not been found in association with extinct fauna, and the only site that has been dated by the radiocarbon method, the Bull Brook site in Massachusetts, was occupied about 7000 B.C. (Byers, 1954, 1959).[2] Another protégé of J. Alden Mason has undertaken investigations that have thrown new light on the probable age of Eastern fluted points. Ronald Mason has found that studies of distribution as related to paleogeography suggest an essentially comparable age for fluted points in the East and for the Western Clovis points (Mason, 1962). Geological evidence from Western sites suggests an age of between 8000 and 10,000 B.C. for Clovis points. Twelve radiocarbon dates from six sites cluster around 9300 B.C.

Students of Early Man are very conscious of the Pennsylvania area because of the Shoop site, near Enterline, Pennsylvania, which produced the assemblage of artifacts, including fluted points, called the Enterline Chert Industry. John Witthoft, who described the industry, provided valuable data concerning techniques of manufacture, and tools and implements other than projectile points (Witthoft, 1952).

Throughout the Eastern United States there has been increasing interest in cultures of the preceramic Archaic stage. Many sites have been found that bear evidence of the presence of hunting and gathering groups who hunted a wide variety of game and utilized many vegetal foods, and in some areas depended heavily on shellfish. They used some unfluted lanceolate points and many notched and stemmed forms. Tools of the early Archaic were produced by flak-

[2] The Debert site, a fluted point site near Truro, Nova Scotia, has produced a series of radiocarbon dates that cluster around 8600 B.C.

ing, and unflaked implements and utensils were shaped by use rather than design. Grinding and polishing techniques came into use during the later part of the Archaic. It was originally believed that the Archaic sites were far younger than those of the Paleo-Indian stage. However, radiocarbon dates from sites in Alabama, Illinois, and Missouri, indicate that there was occupation by Archaic peoples as early as 7000 and 8000 B.C. (Logan, 1952, Fowler, 1959).

Among the most important developments in the area that lies to the west of the Rocky Mountains is the recognition of a variety of manifestations of a tradition to which the name "Desert Culture" is often applied. A great deal of information has been derived from Danger Cave, a stratified site in Utah where occupation began in the ninth millennium B.C. (Jennings, 1957). Also of major importance are the sites of the Cochise Culture of the Southwest (Sayles and Antevs, 1941). There is no evidence that the Desert Culture is an outgrowth of the big game hunting culture that produced fluted points. These would seem to represent two different traditions. Desert Culture people did some hunting, using stemmed and notched projectile points, but the rigors of the environment led to a strong dependence on plant foods as well. Choppers and keeled and domed scrapers were characteristic tools. Milling stones came into use at a very early period, perhaps by 8000 B.C. Basketry was also early here, and was being produced in the seventh millennium B.C.

Basketry and sandals were equally early in the Northwestern United States. The whole area ranging from the Yukon coast to southern Oregon and extending westward into Idaho is character-ized at the earliest level, beginning somewhere around 9000 B.C., by the use of biface leaf-shaped points. Notched forms came in at an early period. Some of the most important investigations in this area have been sponsored by the American Philosophical Society. Nota-ble among these are the investigations in the Klamath Lake area and at the Dalles on the Oregon side of the Columbia River (Cress-man, 1956, 1960).

Bipointed leaf-shaped points are found in the Arctic, in various parts of the United States, and in Mexico, where they are often called Lerma points. In a site near Tamaulipas such points were found in an horizon dated by the radiocarbon method at 7315 B.C. (MacNeish, 1958). These investigations were also sponsored by the

American Philosophical Society. Similar points were discovered in the Valley of Mexico in association with mammoth (Aveleyra, 1956).

Leaf-like forms are the predominant type in preceramic contexts in South America. They are of different varieties, and some may be relatively recent, but others are undoubtedly quite ancient. The extraordinarily wide distribution of this type through two continents is of interest, for this simple, indeterminate form appears to have been the only type of projectile point that was available for export from Siberia prior to the Neolithic, and it may well be the prototype from which the more specialized American forms developed. Fluting is undoubtedly a New World development.

Although much has been learned about the implements of the Paleo-Indians, we know regrettably little about the people who made them, for there has been a great dearth of ancient human bones. Only one partial human skeleton, found near Midland, Texas, is widely accepted as of Paleo-Indian age (Wendorf, Krieger, Albritton, Stewart, 1955). There is, however, one human bone, a fragmentary pelvis, which has been in Philadelphia since 1845 and which is still in the collections of the Academy of Natural Sciences, that may be some 11,000 years old (Richards, 1951). This bone was found near Natchez, Mississippi, in a fossil bone bed that contained the remains of mastodon and extinct ground sloth, horse, and bison. Although fluorine tests run in 1895 indicated that the human pelvis and a sloth bone were of the same age, it was not until 1951 that these almost forgotten studies were brought to the attention of anthropologists by T. D. Stewart. Fluorine cannot provide evidence of exact age, it can only show contemporaneity of bones. The evidence available, however, suggests that a date of about 9000 B.C. would be of the right order of magnitude for the Natchez pelvis.

We are still faced with many major problems. Perhaps the most important is the need to determine when man first entered this hemisphere. We know that by 8000 B.C. different cultural traditions were established in different parts of the Americas, and that man had reached Patagonia. Some time must surely have elapsed since the first entry into the New World. It is unlikely that American prehistorians would seriously question an estimate of some 15,000 years ago (13,000 B.C.), but new evidence suggests that this may not be early enough.

Unfortunately, the Lewisville, Texas site, which had yielded the earliest radiocarbon date, indicating an age in excess of 35,000 B.C., has not provided incontrovertible evidence, and the site is now inundated (Crook and Harris, 1957). The Tule Springs locality in Nevada, with a radiocarbon date of about 26,000 B.C., is fortunately still available (Harrington and Simpson, 1961). A very large-scale, interdisciplinary project, under the direction of Richard Shutler, was initiated on October 1, 1962.[3]

Another locality of major importance is the Valsequillo gravel area near Puebla, Mexico, where investigations by Juan Armenta and Cynthia Irwin, aided by the American Philosophical Society, have revealed associations of artifacts and extinct fauna in what appears to be an early context. This area too is still available for further work, and additional excavations should certainly be undertaken.

There is also an interesting series of discoveries of crude uniface implements on high terraces in various localities in California (Harrington and Simpson, 1961). It is unwise to place too great a dependence on typology, since early forms appear to have persisted later in America than in some other parts of the world, but a pattern of association with high terraces, which are quite old, could be significant.

Conclusive evidence is not yet available, but the writer is convinced that proof will be found that man was present in the New World at a much earlier period than is now generally accepted.

There is a very great need for habitation sites. So many of our important Early Man sites have been "kill sites," where only projectile points and a few butchering tools are represented, that we have very little knowledge of complete assemblages. The few habitation sites that have been found suggested that some forms and techniques characteristic of the Lower or Middle Paleolithic in

[3] Excavation revealed an extraordinarily complex stratigraphic column which had led to a radiocarbon sampling from two deposits of different ages. It now appears that man came into this area between 11,000 and 9,000 B.C. Archaeological evidence was scanty and consisted of only one stone scraper, five flakes, and three polished bone objects which may be tools.

Western Europe persisted here for a far longer time, continuing into periods that would be equated with the Upper Paleolithic and Mesolithic. We need to know much more about the lithic technology of the Western Hemisphere.

A great deal remains to be learned about the preceramic cultures of South America. We cannot solve our problems by thinking only in terms of one continent. Actually, it is not enough to think only in terms of one hemisphere. It is highly desirable that we learn a great deal more about the archaeology of eastern Siberia, since it is believed that man first entered the Western Hemisphere by way of Bering Strait. Syntheses of Siberian data such as those which Henry Michael of Temple University has produced are of major importance (Michael, 1958). The contributions of Dr. Rainey should also be noted. He was the first American archaeologist to visit the Soviet Union and make contact with Soviet archaeologists. The fine impression that he made and the rapport which he established were of paramount importance in arranging for later visits by other American archaeologists. Those of us who have gone there since and received fine cooperation have profited greatly.

Studies of Siberian Paleolithic collections have not revealed any one complex that may be regarded as the source of the Paleo-Indian cultures of the New World. It has become apparent, however, that certain elements characteristic of the Siberian Paleolithic are present in New World cultures. These include chopping tools that resemble those of southeast Asia, keeled and discoidal scrapers and flake implements that resemble Mousterian types, somewhat crude blades, and bifacially flaked leaf-shaped points. The latter were not important in the early Siberian assemblages, but they were present in some (Wormington, 1962).

One very obvious need is for firmly dated human skeletal remains of Pleistocene age. It is not enough to know the tools of the first Americans; we should know something about the people themselves. It would also be desirable to have information about their settlement patterns. The scarcity of human bones and of habitation sites in America may have special significance. The limited number of discoveries and the relative sparseness of artifacts in known Paleo-Indian sites is one of the first things that strikes European observers. Granted, there has been a much longer period of occupation in the

Old World, but when comparisons are made on the same level between America on the one hand and Europe and Africa on the other, it would appear that there may have been a considerable disparity in population density.

In the Eastern United States much work remains to be done in determining the nature of the relationship between the stage characterized by fluted points and the so-called Archaic. There is inadequate stratigraphic evidence and a paucity of radiocarbon dates. Are these really two sequent stages, as is currently believed by most archaeologists, or could they be two different traditions which were in part contemporaneous? It would also be highly desirable to seek to determine the meaning of the similarities that exist between Archaic lithic assemblages of the East and those of the Desert Culture of the West.

Although many questions remain concerning the Paleo-Indians, it is certain that some important answers will be found in the not too distant future. On the basis of the past record, it would seem perfectly safe to wager that members of the Philadelphia Anthropological Society and institutions in the Philadelphia area will be helping to provide those answers.

REFERENCES

Agogino, George A. (1961). "A New Point Type from Hell Gap Valley, Eastern Wyoming," *American Antiquity*, 26, No. 4, pp. 258–60.
———(1962). Personal communication.
Agogino, George A., and W. D. Frankforter (1960). "The Brewster Site: An Agate Basin Folsom Multiple Component Site in Eastern Wyoming," *The Master Key*, Southwest Museum, 34, No. 3, pp. 102–7.
Aveleyra Arroyo de Anda, Luis (1956). "The Second Mammoth and Associated Artifacts at Santa Isabel Iztapan," *American Antiquity*, 22, No. 1, pp. 12–28.
Byers, Douglas S. (1954). "Bull Brook—A Fluted Point Site in Ipswich, Massachusetts," *American Antiquity*, 19, No. 4, pp. 342–51.
———(1959). "Radiocarbon dates for the Bull Brook Site, Massachusetts," *American Antiquity*, 24, No. 4, pp. 427–29.
Cook, Harold J. (1927). "New Geological and Palaeontological Evidence

Bearing on the Antiquity of Mankind in America," *Natural History*, 27, No. 3, pp. 240–47.

Cotter, John L. (1937). "The Occurrence of Flints and Extinct Animals in Pluvial Deposits near Clovis, New Mexico. Pt. IV, Report on the Excavations at the Gravel Pit in 1936," Philadelphia Academy of Natural Sciences, *Proceedings*, 89, pp. 2–16.

———(1938). "The Occurrence of Flints and Extinct Animals in Pluvial Deposits near Clovis, New Mexico. Pt. VI, Report on Field Season of 1937," Philadelphia Academy of Natural Sciences, *Proceedings*, 90, pp. 113–17.

Cressman, L. S. (1956). "Klamath Prehistory," Appendices by William G. Haag and William S. Laughlin. American Philosophical Society, *Transactions*, 46, Part 4.

———(1960). "Cultural Sequence at the Dalles, Oregon," American Philosophical Society, *Transactions*, 50, Part 10.

Crook, William S., Jr., and R. K. Harris (1957). "Hearths and Artifacts of Early Men near Lewisville, Texas, and Associated Faunal Material," *Texas Archaeological Society Bulletin*, 28, pp. 7–97.

Figgins, J. D. (1927). "The Antiquity of Man In America," *Natural History*, 27, No. 3, pp. 229–39.

———(1933). "A Further Contribution to the Antiquity of Man In America," Colorado Museum of Natural History, *Proceedings*, 12, No. 2.

Fowler, Melvin L. (1959). "Summary Report of Modoc Rock Shelter," *Illinois State Museum Report of Investigations*, 8.

Giddings, J. L., Jr., (1951). "The Denbigh Flint Complex," *American Antiquity*, 16, No. 3, pp. 193–202.

Harrington, Mark, and Ruth DeEtte Simpson (1961). "Tule Springs, Nevada, with other Evidence of Pleistocene Man in North America," *Southwest Museum Papers*, No. 18.

Haynes, Vance and George Agogino (1960). "Geological Significance of a New Radiocarbon Date from the Lindenmeier Site," Denver Museum of Natural History, *Proceedings*, No. 9.

Howard, Edgar B. (1935a). "Evidence of Early Man in North America," *The Museum Journal*, University of Pennsylvania Museum, 24, Nos. 2–3.

———(1935b). "Occurrence of Flints and Extinct Animals in Pluvial Deposits near Clovis, New Mexico, Pt. 1, Introduction," Philadelphia Academy of Natural Sciences, *Proceedings*, 87, pp. 299–303.

Howard, Edgar B., Linton Satterthwaite, Jr., and Charles Bache (1941).

"Preliminary Report on a Buried Yuma Site in Wyoming," *American Antiquity*, 7, No. 1, pp. 70–74.

Jennings, Jesse D. (1957). "Danger Cave," Society for American Archaeology, *Memoirs*, No. 14.

Jepsen, Glenn L. (1951). "Ancient Buffalo Hunters in Wyoming," Archaeological Society of New Jersey, *News Letter* No. 24, pp. 22–24.

———(1953). "Ancient Buffalo Hunters," *Princeton Alumni Weekly*, 53, No. 25, pp. 10–12.

Logan, Wilfred D. (1952). "Graham Cave, An Archaic Site in Montgomery County, Missouri," Missouri Archaeological Society, *Memoir* No. 2.

MacNeish, Richard S. (1958). "Investigations in the Sierra de Tamaulipas, Mexico," American Philosophical Society, *Transactions*, 48, Part 6.

Mason, Ronald J. (1962). "The Paleo-Indian Tradition in Eastern North America," *Current Anthropology*, 3, No. 3, pp. 227–46.

Michael, Henry N. (1958). "The Neolithic Age in Eastern Siberia," American Philosophical Society, *Transactions*, 48, Part 2.

Moss, John H. (1951). (in collaboration with Kirk Bryan, G. William Holmes, Linton Satterthwaite, Jr., Henry P. Hansen, C. Bertrand Schultz, W. D. Frankforter) "Early Man in the Eden Valley," *Museum Monographs*, The University Museum, University of Pennsylvania.

Rainey, Froelich (1940) "Archaeological Investigations in Central Alaska," *American Antiquity*, 5, No. 4, pp. 299–308.

Richards, Horace G. (1951). "The Vindication of Natchez Man," *Frontiers*, 15, No. 5, pp. 139–40. Philadelphia Academy of Natural Sciences.

Roberts, Frank H. H. Jr. (1935). "A Folsom Complex: Preliminary Report on Investigations at the Lindenmeier Site in Northern Colorado," *Smithsonian Miscellaneous Collections*, 94.

———(1936). "Additional Information on the Folsom Complex: Report on the Second Season's Investigations at the Lindenmeier Site in Northern Colorado," *Smithsonian Miscellaneous Collections*, 95, No. 10.

Satterthwaite, Linton (1957). "Stone Artifacts at and near the Finley Site, near Eden, Wyoming," *Museum Monographs*, The University Museum. University of Pennsylvania.

Sayles, E. B., and Ernst Anters (1941). *The Cochise Culture*, Medallion Papers, No. 16, Gila Pueblo, Globe, Arizona.

Schultz, C. Bertrand, and L. C. Eiseley (1935). "Paleontological Evidence of the Antiquity of the Scottsbluff Basin Quarry and Its Associated

Artifacts," *American Anthropologist*, New Series, 3, No. 2, pp. 306–18.
———(1936). "An Added Note on the Scottsbluff Quarry," *American Anthropologist*, 3, No. 3, pp. 521–24.

Wendorf, Fred, Alex D. Krieger, Claude C. Albritton, and T. D. Stewart (1955). *The Midland Discovery*, University of Texas Press.

Witthoft, John (1952). "A Paleo-Indian Site in Eastern Pennsylvania: An Early Hunting Culture," *Proceedings American Philosophical Society*, 96, No. 4, pp. 464–95.

Wormington, H. M. (1962). "The Problems of the Presence and Dating in America of Flaking Techniques Similar to the Palaeolithic in the Old World," *Atti del VI Congresso Internazionale delle Scienze Preistoriche e Protostoriche*, Roma. Vol. 1, Relazioni Generali, pp. 273–83.

GORDON F. EKHOLM

Mesoamerican Archaeology

IT NEED hardly be pointed out that Middle America is an extraordinarily attractive field for archaeological research. The physical remains of an ancient civilization are extremely abundant, and the collections in the University of Pennsylvania Museum provide ample evidence that in sculpture, ceramics, and painting these remains are often of exceptional aesthetic quality. There is a strange but impressive architecture, be it in the grandiose pyramidal clusters of Mexico or the, to us, more understandable "buildings" of the Maya. The attraction for the archaeologist has derived also from the fact that the civilization represented by these objects and ruins is mysterious—in that it is largely unknown through written records. The descriptions and historical accounts provided by the sixteenth-century Spaniards are notably fragmentary and do not reach very far back into the past. Furthermore, the one portion of Middle America that is best revealed in these written records is that of the Central Mexican Aztecs, and theirs was a particularly bizarre culture that has excited historians and social scientists since it first became known to the Western World.

It is fortunate that the documentation and study of ancient Middle America was pursued as diligently as it was by the Spanish friars of the sixteenth century, or we would be far more in the dark than we are. This was followed, however, by little interest in Middle America's past in the seventeenth and eighteenth centuries, and it wasn't until near the middle of the nineteenth century that intellectual interest was again focused on Middle America. John Lloyd Stephens was then largely instrumental in drawing attention to the Maya ruins while others were exploring and publishing descriptions of the varied ancient remains of Mexico. The latter half of the nineteenth century saw a renaissance of interest in the pre-Columbian past on the part of Mexican historians, and Daniel G. Brinton, who must be considered one of the major forces in establishing anthropological interests in the intellectual life of Philadelphia, was actively collecting and studying linguistic and historical materials of Middle America. This led in the 1890s into the modern period of many-sided scientific investigation into the history of the area.

It would have been of interest, perhaps, if I had chosen to attempt tracing the history of exploration and of the intellectual currents that have directed the research that has been done in Middle America in the last sixty years. This would have given me the opportunity of stressing the importance of the role that has been played by the institutions and the many individuals of Philadelphia, but this history is ground that has been recently traversed by Ignacio Bernal (1952a, 1952b) and by Gordon Willey (1961). I have chosen rather to limit my comments to only certain aspects of the history of Middle American research and to use these in exploring a trend in our thinking that seems to me to be of particular significance.

One of the interests of recent years has been the attempt to define more precisely what is meant by the word "civilization" when applied to the ancient cultures of Middle America. It is now generally understood that we use the word civilization in a classificatory sense, as referring to something more complex and more advanced than the so-called primitive or indigenous cultures of the world. Although the peoples of Middle America did not have a really effective system of writing, which is considered in some quarters to be the criterion of what may be called civilization, they did have the large populations, complex religious systems, class-structured societies, and in some places, at least, the urban groupings or cities that are characteristic of what in the overall development of human society we know as civilization—or what in this context we might best call early civilization.

Another important development of the last several decades has been the adoption of the concept of Mesoamerica, first proposed by Kirchhoff (1943). Mesoamerica is not just a synonym for Middle America. It refers to the high cultures of Mexico and northern Central America, and excludes the simpler cultures of the northern arid regions of Mexico and the cultures of southern Central America that are basically related to those of South America. Part of the concept of Mesoamerica is that all of the peoples within this area shared certain basic traits and that we can think of it as a culture area despite the cultural variations that do occur. Another part of the concept is that this is a culture area with time depth, and we think of Mesoamerican civilization as beginning about 1500 B.C. and continuing to the European conquest in 1520—thus having a life span of 3000 years.

These brief definitions of terms have been given, for I wish to comment on two aspects of the archaeology of Mesoamerican civilization. Both of them have to do with interareal or intercultural relationships, the first with interregional relationships within Mesoamerica, and the second with relationships between Mesoamerica and the world outside.

Much of the work in American archaeology has been done by specialists in particular regions or areas, and this specialization has often resulted in a kind of aggregate presenting—what seems to me a rather myopic view of culture history. There has been a long period when we have thought of each area as being pretty much isolated from happenings in other areas. It was particularly true of the Maya-ists, for example, some of whom twenty years ago could think of Maya history as being a tight little entity all by itself. This isolationist view has gradually broken down, however, and we see that the larger unit of Mesoamerica has come into being.

We have come to think of Mesoamerica as a single culture area or as a co-tradition that is composed of a number of centers, regions, or foci of partially unique cultural developments. As outlined in a previous paper (Ekholm, 1958), these centers can be identified as those of the Lowland Maya, the Highland Maya, the Zapotec-Mixtec center in Oaxaca, the vital culture center of Central Mexico, and, along the eastern Gulf Coast, the three separate units of the Huasteca, Central Vera Cruz, and the important and early culture center of the ancient Olmec. Each of these centers or regions had to a greater or lesser degree its own distinctive culture tradition, or at least what we might define as its own particular or diagnostic style. The Lowland Maya used the corbelled arch, for instance, and recorded their particularly detailed hieroglyphic inscriptions on large stone stelae; but these traits are completely absent in the nearby Highland Maya region, as they are for the most part elsewhere in Mesoamerica. To varying degrees we have these marked style differences between regions despite the basic cultural uniformities that existed. We have realized that there must have been intercommunication between the regions to account for their basic similarities, but at the same time we have thought of these several regions as having been semi-isolated to account for their differences.

While this conception of Mesoamerica has been in the process of clarification, we have also been coming to the conclusion—through other avenues of inquiry—that the general level of cultural development in Mesoamerica did reach a stage we can call civilization, as has been mentioned above. What, then, does this stage of development imply with regard to the degree of intercommunication that we can suppose existed within Mesoamerica?

The thesis I would like to present is that we must think of Mesoamerica, far more than we have in the past, as a single large interrelated community. This is because it would seem that the several parts of Mesoamerica were undoubtedly linked and interlinked with trade routes and other lines of communication to a far greater extent than can be documented by actual trade objects found archaeologically, or by the meager historical documents available. In my opinion there was probably more intercommunication between regions than we find postulated in most attempts at reconstructing or visualizing the nature of Mesoamerican society.

The high degree of complexity of Mesoamerican civilization that is becoming apparent through archaeology presupposes that in many of the great centers we would undoubtedly have found numerous full-time artists and political and religious specialists. It is more than probable that such specialists would have taken a lively interest in foreign regions and that there must have been a great deal of travel back and forth. Embassies doubtlessly traveled to distant centers for political alliances, trade negotiations, and for many other reasons. Magicians, musicians, or groups of actors probably wandered about from center to center, and on certain occasions skilled artists were probably brought from one center to another to provide special services. I mentioned actors, for, in another early civilization, for which we have some written accounts, such travels are recorded. Thus we have record of a group of Syrian jugglers that in Roman times (121 A.D.) got as far distant from home as central China

(Needham, 1954, p. 197). For about the same date there are other accounts of merchants who made the same lengthy journey and returned home again. Perhaps the cultural situation was different in many ways in Asia, but we must expect that events more or less comparable to these must have occurred in Mesoamerica.

The usual practice in archaeology is to postulate intercommunication between regions only when concrete evidence of influence is visible in changing artifact styles or when actual trade objects are found. Due to the always incomplete nature of the archaeological record, however, the number of trade objects that are found must be only a very limited indication of the degree of intercommunication that was probably taking place.

The difficulty of inferring by archaeological means alone the degree of intercommunication that must have existed in one instance is illustrated, to some extent, by the Aztec tribute records. These are an accounting of vast amounts of material goods that the Aztec demanded periodically from their many subject peoples located throughout much of central and southern Mexico. To some extent this close relationship would be apparent archaeologically if a number of late Aztec sites were very extensively and carefully excavated, but the evidence would never indicate the amount of tribute collected or the continual contacts that this implies. This is due to the fact that the tribute was to a very large proportion in the form of perishable materials, such as foodstuffs, textiles, feathers, and paper. Objects of metal and stone are included in small numbers, but it is of interest to note that quotas of pottery—the material that is given so much emphasis as an archaeological yardstick—are of minor importance in these lists. Mention is made of one form of yellow-colored pottery that the Aztecs claimed as tribute from the west, and tribute in honey is pictured as being supplied in large jars. It is obvious, however, that the widespread and far-reaching political and economic activities of Aztec Mexico that are known to us by means of the written sources could never be reconstructed or appreciated by archaeological means alone.

It is possible, of course, that the range of kinds and quantities of materials demanded by the capital of an empire might be somewhat different from what we could expect to have passed from group to group in more ordinary processes of trade, but it is probable that the differences would not be too great. When, therefore, for pre-Aztec periods we find certain pottery styles, such as Plumbate and Thin Orange, distributed widely throughout Mesoamerica, we must assume, I believe, that great quantities of other materials that leave no archaeological traces were also being carried back and forth to all parts of the area.

Speculations on the nature of the political-economic systems of the Classic Period have tended to be that these were somewhat different from what they were in the post-Classic. Undoubtedly there were differences, but it is probable that, in the main, the basic forms of these systems did not change materially through time. The differences that have seemed to exist are due largely to the fact that those of the post-Classic are known historically while those of the Classic are known only through archaeology. Our view of the latter is clouded by our, as yet, inadequate methods of interpreting archaeological records. Space does not permit a full discussion of this idea, but it is my impression that the Classic Period had its widespread tribute empires similar in kind to that of the Aztec. It is probable, too, that the systems of long distance trade known to exist in Aztec times (Chapman, 1957) can be postulated for the Classic Period as well.

This great amount of trade and other intercommunication, that I believe should be inferred for all of Mesoamerica, would have led, of course, to rather complete knowledge among at least the upper classes in any one region of what was happening in other regions. It seems most probable, for instance, that the elite of Teotihuacan would have known precisely what was happening at Tikal or at Monte Alban—that Princess Ix bacal, let us say, was marrying into the ruling family of Uaxactun, or that the house of Zachil was momentarily in a state of crisis because of the continued drought! This intercommunication and the flow of gossip and knowledge would undoubtedly become altered from time to time due to particular political events or warfare, but such disruptions would not long interfere with the everyday affairs of merchants and markets and the interest in knowing what was happening elsewhere.

Following this line of reasoning, our conception would have to be that no part of Mesoamerica was really isolated from any other. This includes the Lowland Maya whose culture during the Classic

Period has long been considered ingrown and remote but whose participation in the whole Mesoamerican community is becoming more and more evident—especially as the results come in from the University Museum's excavations at Tikal. The Tlaloc figures, the abundant Teotihuacan style pottery, and the jade mask that looks as if it were in the Guerrero Olmec tradition, that have recently come to light there, are material evidence for this view. It is these extensive although costly excavations of major sites that are of especial importance to our understanding of those aspects of Mesoamerican history we are considering here. They provide information that will not come from any other kind of archaeological undertaking.

There is the important question, however, of how this conception of widespread intercommunication within Mesoamerica can be made compatible with the obvious fact that we find definite style areas that remained distinct over long periods of time. The answer appears to be that these styles remained distinct in spite of the close relationship between regions. The political pattern in Mesoamerica was not one that demanded cultural uniformity, and local cultural entities were apparently not forced out of existence. It is of interest, too, to look to foreign areas for comparable situations, and among these the Near East is perhaps revealing. There we find enough written history to learn that Egypt and Mesopotamia, as well as other centers of the eastern Mediterranean, were highly cognizant of each other's accomplishments through extensive trade and other kinds of contacts, and exchanged ideas quite freely. Each region retained its own distinctive character, however—its own architectural forms, pottery styles, burial practices, writing, and many other things. These did not diffuse throughout the larger area, and the differences between Egyptian, Mesopotamian, and Minoan art and civilization are about equal in kind and degree to those that distinguish Monte Alban, Tajin, and Piedras Negras.

While what we are thinking of as Mesoamerica was an area that was especially closely integrated among its several parts or regions, it was certainly not a closed system. It was only a part of the whole cultural panorama of the New World and it is becoming more apparent all the time that our previously held views of completely isolated cultural islands are not a true picture of the situation.

A major problem is that of what degree of intercommunication or relationship existed between Mesoamerica and the civilization of the Andean area of South America. This is a subject that has been receiving special attention in recent years, and the evidence is growing that considerable intercommunication did occur at various times, confirming my suspicion that it was much more extensive than is commonly thought.

Muriel Porter (1953) was the first to itemize elements and traits and to clearly establish probable linkages between the pottery complex of the pre-Classic site of Tlatilco in the Valley of Mexico and that of Chavin-Cupisnique in Peru. Clifford Evans and Betty Meggers have been struck by the resemblances between the figurine art of Ecuador and that of Mexico that was first mentioned long ago by Uhle and then discredited. Also, their establishment of a long cultural sequence in Ecuador coincided with the work of Michael Coe at La Victoria on the coast of Guatemala in Mesoamerica, and the latter has made a good case for connections between the two areas by sea travel—1500 miles along a difficult coast (Coe, 1960). Alfred Kidder of the University Museum, whose interests cover both Mesoamerica and the Andes, has just recently suggested that some of the similarities between Olmec art and that of Chavin in Peru may best be explained by another set of sea voyages.

In the other direction, we have seen a rapidly growing interest in the problems of relationships between Mesoamerica and the Southwestern United States. Intensive work in Durango by J. C. Kelly and extensive excavations by Di Peso at Casas Grandes have clarified the diffusional picture in northern Mexico, but the conclusion seems to be that the scattered Mexican elements that appear during various phases in the Southwest were probably in the main brought by traders or travelers and cannot be fully accounted for by a slow site-to-site diffusional mechanism. No one has commented recently on connections between Mesoamerica and the Southeastern United States, but, in my opinion, we probably will find that fairly frequent travel by either Mexicans or Southeasterners across the archaeologically empty area of northeastern Mexico and coastal Texas separating the two areas must have occurred to account for the many Mexican elements that appeared at various times in the Southeast.

I have recently shown that the enigmatic stone collars of Puerto Rico are probably ball-game belts, similar in use to the stone yokes of Mexico (Ekholm, 1961). This, with the ball-courts of the island which are best known through the work of J. Alden Mason (1941), indicate extensive contact between Mesoamerica and the islands. These are contacts that do not seem to be revealed in the ceramics or other artifacts of the two regions.

Finally, to go even farther afield, there is the problem of relationships between Mesoamerica and the civilizations of Asia—of China and India—and of their possible significance to happenings in America. This is a special problem, however, and can be no more than mentioned at this time. It requires intensive research before the suspicions we have can be validated, but if another "probably" is to be permitted, I would say that the civilizations of the New World are probably not so isolated from those of the Old World as we have thought.

The ideas I have been presenting here concern our conceptions, as archaeologists, of the nature of Mesoamerican civilization, or, more specifically, of the processes of cultural diffusion that operated in these societies. I have necessarily been brief and I have ventured into the realm of speculation in a manner that will not be everywhere acceptable, but I have wanted to emphasize my belief that theoretical considerations of the processes of cultural diffusion have been woefully neglected in our thinking and writing in the field of American archaeology.

These are not entirely new ideas. There is a general trend toward a loosening up, as it were, of our conception of how cultures or cultural traits can and did diffuse, and of how the New World cultures were indeed the traditions of human beings—not just abstractions, such as pottery types, in the minds of archaeologists. Further progress in this direction will play an important role in the future development of our understanding of the American past.

REFERENCES

Bernal, Ignacio (1952a). "Cien Años de Arqueologia Mexicana, 1780–1880." *Cuadernos Americanos,* Mexico, Año 11, No. 2, pp. 137–51.
———(1952b). "La Arqueologia Mexicana de 1880 a La Fecha." *Cuadernos Americanos,* Mexico, Año 11, No. 5, pp. 121–45.

Chapman, Anne C. (1957). "Port of Trade Enclaves in Aztec and Maya Civilizations," in Karl Polanyi, Conrad M. Arensberg, and Harry W. Pearson, eds., *Trade and Market in the Early Empires* (New York, The Free Press), pp. 114–53.

Coe, Michael D. (1960). "Archaeological Linkages with North and South America at La Victoria, Guatemala," *American Anthropologist*, 62, No. 3, pp. 363–93.

Ekholm, Gordon F. (1958). "Regional Sequences in Mesoamerica and Their Relationships," in *Middle American Anthropology*, Special Symposium of the American Anthropological Association. Pan American Union, Social Science Monographs, 5, pp. 15–24.

———(1961). "Puerto Rican Stone 'Collars' as Ball-game Belts," S. K. Lothrop, et al., *Essays in Pre-Columbian Art and Archaeology* (Cambridge, Harvard University Press), pp. 356–71.

Kirchhoff, Paul (1943). "Mesoamerica," *Acta Americana*, 1, No. 1, pp. 92–107.

Mason, J. Alden (1941). "A Large Archaeological Site at Capá, Utuado, with Notes on other Porto Rican Sites visited in 1914–1915," The New York Academy of Sciences, *Scientific Survey of Porto Rico and the Virgin Islands*, 18, Part 2.

Needham, Joseph (1954). *Science and Civilization in China*, Vol. 1 (Cambridge, England, Cambridge University Press).

Porter, Muriel N. (1953). *Tlatilco and the Pre-Classic Cultures of the New World*. Viking Fund Publications in Anthropology, No. 19 (New York, The Viking Fund, Inc.).

Willey, Gordon R. (1961). "Developments in the Archaeology of Nuclear America, 1935–60," *American Antiquity*, 27, No. 1, pp. 46–55.

CHESTER S. CHARD

Arctic Anthropology
in America[1]

OUR FOCUS today is to be upon current trends—which I take to mean the developments of the postwar years leading up to the picture as seen at the present moment. However, I cannot pass over in silence the important contributions which Philadelphia anthropologists have made to Northern studies in earlier years. We can point to Hallowell's classic study of circumpolar bear ceremonialism; Davidson on snowshoes; De Laguna's pioneer field work in southern Alaska (excavations at Cook Inlet in 1930, and three years later in Prince William Sound, along with ethnographic studies of the Chugach Eskimo and the hitherto unknown Eyak—followed in 1935 by an adventuresome reconnaissance of the Yukon River). The work of Frank G. Speck I have left to Dr. Eggan, but let me at least note his incidental papers on the Labrador Eskimo. During the 1930s one of the most prominent figures on the Alaskan scene was Froelich Rainey, who contributed significantly to our knowledge of the early periods on St. Lawrence Island, pioneered in the search for traces of early man in interior Alaska, and wound up in a blaze of glory for his role in the discovery and excavation of the sensational Ipiutak site. (This is not to slight his exploits as a member of an Eskimo whaling crew at Point Hope.) A conspicuous feature of the campus landscape at the University of Alaska, Rainey Ridge, serves to remind later generations of the part he played in establishing

[1] The writer is greatly indebted to the following colleagues, who placed their information and viewpoints at his disposal: Ronald Cohen, Charles Hughes, W. S. Laughlin, Catharine McClellan, Verne Ray, Ivar Skarland and James VanStone. The interpretations offered here are, however, the writer's alone, and are not to be ascribed to any of the above. The text stands as written in 1962, with added citations to a few major works published through 1966.

anthropology at the only institution of higher learning in the American Arctic.

The University Museum's interest in the North is also of long standing. One could recall the Siberian expedition of 1914–1915 to the lower Yenisei; the many years during which Louis Shotridge, a member of the Chilkat Tlingit group, was connected with the museum and was responsible for securing some of its finest specimens; the acquisition of the Van Valin collection of archaeological materials from Point Barrow; and J. Alden Mason's own 1913–1914 ethnological field work among the Athabascan groups near Great Slave Lake.

As we turn our attention now to the postwar period, it is obvious that persons associated with or trained in Philadelphia institutions are continuing to play a major role in the Arctic field. One need only mention such names as Frederica De Laguna, J. L. Giddings, Catharine McClellan, James VanStone, Edmund Carpenter, Henry Michael, Norman Chance, or W. S. Laughlin (who holds his Sigma Xi key from Bryn Mawr), in order to suggest the range and magnitude of their contributions.

I obviously cannot attempt anything approaching a complete survey of the work accomplished in the North during the past fifteen years. I will therefore restrict myself to American and Canadian research only, and define the Arctic for present purposes as the areas occupied by the Eskimo-Aleut stock (excluding Greenland, the private hunting preserve of our Danish colleagues), and in addition those occupied by the Northern Athabascans and their Tlingit kinsmen; there will also be brief excursions into Siberia. I shall content myself, under the circumstances, with mentioning the highlights in the record of accomplishment and singling out what I feel are the most significant developments and trends over the postwar years and at the present time. This will be, then, an impressionistic overview, painted with broad strokes and ignoring much detail and many worthy contributions; it should not be mistaken for a summary of our knowledge of the Arctic.

I have heard it said that most of the work on the living peoples of the North in recent years has had practical motivations and that some verges on the realm of social work. This is perhaps inevitable when much of the field work involved has been promoted and financed by organizations faced with practical problems. Even so, we may expect significant data on culture process to emerge from many of these studies, and certainly most of the anthropologists concerned are not primarily committed to what might be termed welfare work. I think it could be argued, however, that most of the basic research in Arctic anthropology in recent years has been done by the archaeologists, and that they have made the major contribution. For this reason, and also because the largest body of data gathered during this period is archaeological, I have accorded the subject a greater share of attention here.

As a base line, what was the situation of Arctic archaeology just before our review begins? We could say that it was represented by sizable collections from a handful of sites; preservation was unusually good in many cases and hence the archaeological record from such sites was remarkably complete. Methodologically it was characterized by the direct historical approach and a close tie-up with living ethnology. "Our Arctic archaeology . . . first appeared in the light cast by scholarly ethnographers . . . and thus became a functional prehistory of Eskimos." (Giddings 1962a, p. 155) There were those who felt that Eskimo archaeology had been basically worked out by 1941 and that the stage of exploration was past. The prehistory of at least the Western Eskimo was neatly embodied in the St. Lawrence Island sequence, and the many divergent aspects of southern Alaskan Eskimo culture were viewed as the result of Indian influence. However, the archaeology of the vast interior regions was almost a total blank, and there was perhaps a feeling that it would continue to be. In the absence of archaeological evidence here, attempts to probe into the past relied primarily on ethnographic data, and a picture of circumpolar and circumboreal culture flow or shared tradition had been built up (see, e.g., the studies of Hallowell, 1926; Davidson, 1937; De Laguna, 1946, 1947; Cooper, 1946; Spaulding, 1946). Although Siberia was a blank spot archaeologically to most Americans, the first interhemispheric comparisons had produced the Woodland pottery origin hypothesis—which then seemed a daring innovation—and Collins' identification of Eurasian features in the prehistoric period on St. Lawrence Island, leading him to postulate that Eskimo culture was a product of the Old World appearing on the scene about the time of Christ (Collins, 1937). Perhaps the most striking feature of the Alaskan scene was the surprising lack of the expectable early materials—if this area was indeed the beachhead of man in the New World.

The postwar years, from the very beginning, have witnessed revolutionary changes in this picture. There was a rapid expansion of activity in the Arctic. A growth of interest, abetted by phenomenally improved transportation facilities, led to increased field work, including the exploration of hitherto unknown regions—the Barren Grounds and Arctic Archipelago of Canada, the east shore of the Bering Sea, the Tlingit territory, and especially the interior wilderness of the Brooks Range and the vast McKenzie-Yukon area. The introduction of new techniques—radiocarbon dating, dendrochronology, beach ridge dating—made possible great strides in the interpretation of data. The discovery of early sites brought about the greatest change of all and immediately released a major new stream of activity. Nor has this been simply a period of feverish data collection. Attempts at synthesis and interpretation have gone hand in hand with field work, to a degree that other regions might well emulate. But above all we can characterize the postwar years as a period of complication of what had seemed a clear and simple picture.

To touch first on techniques and method: Radiocarbon dating of course became available as a tool for the archaeologist simultaneously in many parts of the world; its effect upon the Arctic was no greater than elsewhere, but this does not diminish the importance of this development. Happily, the University of Pennsylvania Carbon 14 laboratory has selected the Arctic as one of the four areas on which it concentrates its work. As a result, the University has made a significant contribution to Arctic prehistory in the past decade through this alone, since our presently accepted chronological framework for the North is largely based on the careful work of the Philadelphia laboratory, which studies its findings as a group, checked and analyzed for internal consistency in most exemplary fashion (e.g., Rainey and Ralph, 1959). The Arctic samples have presented many problems in connection with material (particularly antler, so commonly submitted) as well as with contamination and uncertain associations. Many of the datings are doubtful, in the opinion of the laboratory, and much more work will certainly be needed before Arctic chronology is on a really sound basis. Meanwhile, it could not be in better hands.

Dendrochronology has been applied more successfully in Alaska than in any area outside of the Southwest. Giddings began his tree-ring studies along the Kobuk River as early as 1940, and by the early 1950s had worked out a sequence running back to 978 A.D. and had utilized this for the dating of archaeological sites.

The most sensational breakthrough, however, has come with the emergence of a new method in the last few years, also pioneered by Giddings—beach ridge dating. Whereas in the past, vertical stratigraphy was the best means available for understanding Arctic time sequences—and often it was not available where most badly needed —this new "horizontal stratigraphy" provides a continuous sequence of cultural succession spanning up to 4500 years at a single locality. These raised beaches were formed by the heaviest seas of successive years, and provided a natural location for Eskimo dwellings close to the ocean. With the passage of time, new beaches form and settlement shifts to the current ocean front. Thus the older beaches with their traces of ancient occupation are found progressively further inland, providing a superb situation for a comparative study of the development of Eskimo culture in areas like northwestern Alaska, where these physiographic conditions obtain (Giddings, 1962a).

Also under the heading of method, we should mention the increasing tendency to extract the maximum amount of information on the life and environment of prehistoric communities by utilizing all types of evidence that may be recovered from a given site. This ecological approach, as it might be termed, ideally involves collaborative field investigation of a locality by several different disciplines—e.g., botany, zoology, geology, and all pertinent branches of anthropology. It is well exemplified by the current Aleut-Konyag project of the University of Wisconsin directed by Laughlin and Reeder (Laughlin and Reeder, 1962).

Equally as important as postwar field work was the appearance of final reports on major prewar undertakings, some long delayed: De Laguna's monumental distribution study (1947) growing out of

her Yukon River field work, and later (1956) her monograph on
Prince William Sound; the 1948 Ipiutak report by Larsen and
Rainey; and Ford's 1959 account of his finds at Point Barrow.
Ipiutak was the first stone dropped into the placid mill pond of
prewar Alaskan archaeology; in many ways the culture is still an
enigma. The ensuing arguments over the "Ipiutak theory" were one
of the more prominent features of the first postwar decade, though
they generated, in retrospect, more heat than light. Briefly, the
theory proposed that this aberrant community represented *the* ancestral Eskimo culture, that it represented a bodily migration from
the lower Ob-Yenisei region of Siberia, and that it reflected an
original inland base for Eskimo culture. As the first postwar attempt
at synthesis, the Ipiutak theory is of historical interest.

The next stir came shortly thereafter with Giddings' discovery of
the stratigraphically early microlithic assemblage at Cape Denbigh,
including the first burins to be found in the New World.[2] This
opened new horizons for Arctic archaeologists, and the prehistoric
scene has been characterized by kaleidoscopic change ever since.

Giddings has continued to push back the time horizons in northwestern Alaska, to discover an astonishing number of new cultures
to fill gaps in the sequence, and to fit known cultures of uncertain
status, such as Ipiutak, into their proper place in the developmental
history of Eskimo culture. Giddings' contribution to Arctic prehistory has been nothing short of revolutionary; much of it has been
the product of work on the beaches at Cape Krusenstern in the past
few years. He may have evidence of early whaling here at an age
approaching that of the fully-developed maritime life of the Aleutians, and has in general revealed a major hearth of Eskimo cultural
development. His work along the Kobuk River is also significant for
our ultimate understanding of the complex problem of coast-interior relationships (e.g., Giddings 1952a, 1962b).[3]

Of all the potentially crucial areas, southwestern Alaska is the
least known. Work is under way here, but little has been published
as yet. Laughlin views it as both the hearth and climax area of the

[2] The final report (Giddings, 1964) is a major contribution to Arctic prehistory.

[3] Giddings' tragic death in December 1964 is an irreparable loss to Arctic
anthropology.

Eskimo, whether from the standpoint of language, culture, or morphology. Here the culture was assembled in recognizable form, and from here it dispersed. The Aleutian populations of 4000 years ago as revealed in the bottom level at Chaluka, Umnak Island, were already accomplished offshore hunters of whales, fur seals, and halibut; their economy and insular habitat presupposes the use of boats as good as those of historic times. There has been no change in the way of life in this area over this span of time: Archaeology reveals only changes in styles. One fact that has been firmly established is that the Aleutian island chain is a cul-de-sac, and has never been a bridge from the Old World. The rich resources of southwest Alaska enabled the growth of the largest aboriginal population bloc in the Arctic. In fact, almost one-third of all Eskimos belonged to the Aleut-Pacific Eskimo group. A prime problem of the area, of course, is to explain the differentiation between Eskimo and Aleut which must have occured here. Laughlin points to the coincidence between the winter ice limit and the Aleut-Eskimo linguistic boundary, which may be significant in this respect, leading to adaptation to ice hunting on one side and open-water resources on the other (Laughlin, 1963).

Rainey had justifiably written off the river valleys of central Alaska as migration routes for early man. In the past decade, it is the Brooks Range, Alaska's last wilderness, that has been revealed as the early habitat and route. A major characteristic of Arctic archaeology at the present, therefore, is the focus of current interest on this region in search of early cultures. The cultural sequence in the Brooks Range has the drawback of being based not upon stratigraphy or seriation but only on typology and comparisons with outside areas. A further difficulty arises from the fact that the definition of the cultural complexes is based on artifacts either found on the surface or in shallow deposits; also, many of the sites are relatively close together with possibilities of mixture. In the Anaktuvuk Pass area, no less than nine district cultural components have been identified by Campbell alone. The supposed earliest complex (Kogruk) is thought to be one of the oldest traces of human occupation yet discovered anywhere in northern North America. His later Kayuk site, assignable to the "Yuma" tradition with Plains affinities, is one of the largest Paleo-Indian *occupation* sites known. Especially significant is Campbell's conclusion that the modern population of the area, the Nunamiut, are recent arrivals from the Arctic coast—a conclusion that demolishes the much publicized thesis that they are the survivors of a "Paleo-Eskimo" interior population.

It seemed for a while that the necessary stratigraphic key to the placement of such early occupations would be provided by Mac-Neish's Engigstciak site on the Firth River, at the northeast end of the Brooks Range—a strategic spot where any movements are channeled through a narrow funnel as the mountains approach close to the coast. The sequence of nine occupations initially identified promised to be veritable Rosetta Stone of the western Arctic, and great dependence was placed upon it. Unfortunately, further geological studies at the site revealed a complex solifluxion situation which had allowed artifact mixing. The nine complexes are thus poorly defined, and the temporal gaps in the sequence, MacNeish admits, are probably as large as the segments represented (Mac-Neish, 1963).

A less spectacular but more reliable temporal sequence is emerging from MacNeish's most recent excavations at a large number of sites in southern Yukon Territory, five of them stratified. The sequence is confirmed by the soil zone stratigraphy and by the preliminary results of relative dating by the new obsidian hydration method. MacNeish has identified seven distinctive cultural complexes, five of which he believes fall in the period before 1500 B.C. (In the absence of Carbon 14 dates, time estimates are educated guesses). However, he has been unable to close the gap between the microblade tradition and the ancestral Athabascans, so that his historical sequence is not yet a complete picture of Yukon prehistory. Nor is it of immediate use to workers in other areas of the North: lack of close outside parallels makes cross dating difficult (Mac-Neish 1964).

From the methodological standpoint, one of the most important major postwar projects has been De Laguna's long-term program in the Tlingit area, carried out with the able collaboration of Catharine McClellan. This was the first field work in Alaska to combine the knowledge and techniques of personnel trained in several fields of anthropology, so that ethnographic, archaeological, and linguistic approaches were applied to the complex problems of Tlingit cultural history and prehistory. The ultimate aim has been to understand the dynamics of Tlingit culture growth and change, and thereby to gain further insight into the history of culture in northwestern North America. Factors leading to the selection of the Tlingit included the lack of any overall, integrated ethnography of this group; its heterogeneity, including inland and coastal units, and marked local differences; the hope that the northern Tlingit might retain something of the simpler character of early Northwest Coast culture if they were marginal to a southern climax; and the possibility of finding evidence in this area of the postulated long-term cultural exchanges between the Pacific Eskimo and the Northwest Coast. The archaeologists of the project have had meager pickings, suggesting that any population growth in this area is relatively recent. The populous and cultured Tlingit of historic times may thus be a recent development. De Laguna's first published report, "The Story of a Tlingit Community" (1960), is a history of the village of Angoon based on archaeology, oral tradition, and historical data, but it is equally a superb study in method.

Postwar archaeology in the eastern Canadian Arctic has centered on the problem of the Dorset culture (cf., e.g., Taylor, 1959), which has been variously viewed as a migrant Eskimo culture from Alaska, as a Northeastern Archaic Indian population which moved north and became Eskimoized, or (with increasing enthusiasm) as a local development from a proto-Eskimo base. The two most dramatic developments have been the demonstration that the Dorset people were physically Eskimo—ending a long controversy—and the discovery of a succession of sites on old raised beaches in the Igluik area by a joint University of Pennsylvania—Danish National Museum expedition under Meldgaard, that are of fundamental importance to Arctic prehistory. These revealed five stages of Dorset culture, including all known types, in a sort of stratigraphic succession, plus a pre-Dorset manifestation resembling the early Sarqaq of Greenland, but with toggle harpoons that point to a great age for the beginnings of Eskimo culture. The Alarnerk site here is the largest in the eastern Arctic, comprising 208 houses. Previously, only a few certainly Dorset houses had been known anywhere. The still puzzling relationships between the Dorset and the Archaic Indians are being probed by Harp in the southernmost Dorset extension, Newfoundland. If contact did occur, it must have been here where Dorset and Beothuk sites occur in close proximity. Harp's intensive studies also aim at a fuller understanding of Dorset life in all its aspects.

Harp's explorations in the terra incognita of the Barren Grounds have produced interesting results (Harp, 1961). In view of the submergence of this region until relatively recent times and its subsequent uplift, the first human occupation cannot have been much before 3000 B.C., and all coastal remains are those of recent Eskimo. This area has always been marginal from the human standpoint, and not the center of any significant indigenous cultural developments. Since it constitutes one of the more obvious Indian-Eskimo frontier zones, it is of interest that the slight evidence of contact and diffusion is limited to the early pre-Dorset Eskimos. The first occupants of the Barrens were Indians with a Plains-related culture, suggesting northward diffusion of Plains culture in Altithermal times; thereafter, use of the area (which was probably always seasonal) oscillated back and forth between Indian and Eskimo. Of particular significance is Harp's finding that Caribou Eskimo culture has relatively slight archaeological depth, with no clear indication that it was in existence prior to the Thule phase. There is not a shred of evidence to support Birket-Smith's famous hypothesis of a Proto-Eskimo stage with a totally interior culture, whose bearers moved out to the coast to become the classic Central Eskimo. Any interior hunting traditions are clearly associated with Indians. Harp argues plausibly that the ancestral Eskimo cultures (e.g., Denbigh and descendants) "are partial expressions of a dual coastal-interior subsistence economy, now oriented toward the sea, now toward caribou hunting in the back country. . . . This dual adaptation was most certainly a basic aspect of Eskimo life." (Harp, 1961, p. 65) He suggests that when the central Thule economy collapsed, some groups simply moved inland to emphasize the interior aspect of their economy, which now promised more than the sea. Five hundred years of this life would have produced modern Caribou Eskimo culture. Such a view accords with the evidence of linguistics, ethnography, and archaeology (ibid. p. 68).

The status of the enigmatic extinct Sadlermiut of Southampton Island has been a focus of recent interest. Formerly regarded as the last survivors of the Thule culture, they are now believed by Collins to be descendants of the ancient Dorset population, on the basis of trait survivals. As Taylor points out, however, the evident Dorset contributions to the Thule culture may account for the presence of these traits among the Sadlermiut. In any case, there seems no doubt that Sadlermiut culture developed in situ along its own peculiar lines (Taylor, 1959).

The picture of continuous cultural evolution in the eastern Arctic is further strengthened by VanStone's demonstration that the Thule culture is really not as distinctive as Mathiassen made out, and can be shown to have evolved into modern Central Eskimo culture (VanStone, 1962a).

In the realm of postwar theoretical developments, a concern with cultural process began to manifest itself. In 1952, Laughlin had pointed out that "to the extent that both the variability and the structure of Aleut-Eskimo culture have been ignored, the racial poloymorphy unappreciated, the ecological framework disregarded and the time depth minimized, there has been an accompanying lack of attention to process. As a consequence, there has been a frequent resort to migration of unrelated peoples from the most improbable places to explain various traits which were felt to be aberrant. In the study of Eskimo culture as well as in the racial background the underlying assumption that change or evolution took place 'somewhere else' is frequently manifested." (Laughlin, 1952a, p. 25) Yet there is ample evidence of slow internal change over long periods of time in such deep middens as Chaluka and Kukulik—as Collins pointed out in 1937, although his observation appears to have gone largely unheeded. In recent years Giddings has gone so far as to deny any role to migration as a causal factor in major culture change, but Collins points out that there are cases (e.g., the east and west spread of Birnirk) which are best explained by actual population movement (1960, p. 134). It could be added that linguistic homogeneity also speaks for the reality of the Thule migrations, and that documented cases of long journeys by Canadian Eskimos cannot be overlooked.

The older theoretical formulations—e.g., the rigid coast versus inland dichotomy, snowshoe versus ice hunting economy, central Arctic origin for the Eskimo—which had exerted such a strong influence on much prewar thinking, have largely faded away in the light of the new evidence now available. Similarly, the views that much of the richness of southern Bering Sea Eskimo culture is due to Northwest Coast influence, and that the Pacific Eskimo had recently moved down into a formerly Indian area, have been disproved. "The great time depth of Alaskan Eskimo cultures suggests that many ideas concerning the Indian origin of certain traits will have to be revised or abandoned unless greater time depth for the Indian cultures can be found." (Laughlin, 1952b, p. 79)

There has been a growing awareness of St. Lawrence Island as being part of Siberia, with the Alaskan side of the Strait presenting a very different picture. And a northward flow into the Arctic of at least culture traits and techniques from the Plains has been amply demonstrated.

Above all, there has been a marked broadening of the frame of reference, a realization that American Arctic problems cannot be understood unless viewed in a larger context that includes northern Eurasia. This trend owes much to the pioneer efforts of De Laguna. It has led a small number of American students to undertake specific research for the first time on the prehistory of Siberia and adjacent areas of eastern Asia. This American work has focused on two types of activity: making Russian and Japanese findings available in this country through translation programs, summaries, analyses, and bibliographic guides (a good example being the Arctic Institute translation series so ably edited by Henry Michael of Temple University); [4] and secondly the search for Old World origins and relationships of New World cultures and complexes (e.g., early lithic, Eskimo culture, Woodland pottery, and burial mounds) by such scholars as Wormington, Griffin, and Tolstoy. This has included actual study of collections in the Soviet Union as well as analysis of the Russian and Japanese literature, and in this connection we cannot omit mention of the role played by Dr. Rainey in opening up initial contact and communication with our Soviet colleagues.

The several syntheses of Arctic prehistory are of course a significant part of recent theoretical developments. Their specific form and content (readily available and subject to change without no-

[4] See also the COWA publications, *Asian Perspectives, American Antiquity, Abstracts of New World Archaeology, Archives of Archaeology, Arctic Anthropology.*

tice) is of less importance in our overview than the fact that they are being made and altered periodically. Larsen (whom I consider at least an honorary American anthropologist in view of his long association with the University of Alaska), for example, sees Eskimo prehistory in terms of three broad successive culture horizons (Proto-, Paleo-, and Neo-Eskimo) in two major culture areas which produce regional variation (Larsen, 1961).

Giddings views the subject in terms of local development within restricted areas that have their own distinct histories. For instance, in northwest Alaska he distinguishes nine sequential culture horizons (with extensions beyond the area), and through these traces two possible local traditions that seem to represent developmental relationships. To Giddings, "the fabric of Bering Strait archaeology . . . has its warp in the patterns of behavior handed down by parents to their children in a single locality, and a weft made up of the continuous interchange of thoughts outward through space." (1962a, p. 157) His picture is predicated on long-term stability of local populations. The overall picture he summarizes as follows: " . . . it appears that the earliest human leavings yet recognized in the American Arctic are cobble chopper-tools and percussion bifacing followed much later by notched points, then by the microblade-and-burin combinations, then regionally by whaling and deep-house building, then by pottery and the first midden mounds, then by elaboration of engraving art and ceremony, and, finally, by a specialized but utilitarian "Eskimo" form of culture." (1962a, p. 169)

Collins sees three major prehistoric Eskimo traditions—two of them localized, one widespread—and one minor localized tradition. He regards the Denbigh Flint Complex as "perhaps the principal source from which Eskimo culture developed" (1955, p. 186), and manages to cling resolutely to his theory of Mesolithic Eskimo origins by viewing Denbigh as an easterly extension of a widespread Eurasiatic culture of Mesolithic age from which the earliest forms of Eskimo culture are derived. (He receives little support in this from microlithic specialists like Irving, whose analyses indicate an indigenous Alaskan origin for the Arctic Small Tool tradition of which Denbigh is a part.)

Most ambitious of all is MacNeish's attempt (1959) to synthesize the prehistory of all northern North America into a series of ten traditions which have both areal and temporal distribution, forming what he aptly terms a "speculative framework." As he himself readily admits, the sequences have such large gaps, the time estimates are based on such flimsy evidence, and most of the cultures are so poorly known, that the endeavor might be considered reckless rather than merely daring; but we must agree with him wholeheartedly that such attempts must be made if we are to gain any clear picture of relationships in the area. It is MacNeish's suggestion that this series of traditions has spread over large areas of North America in terms of certain ecological zones. Although he thinks that certain elements of each were derived from Asiatic cultures, comparable traditions do not seem to exist in the Old World. Subsequently he has proposed what he calls the "adaptive complex hypothesis" for the peopling of the New World (Mac-Neish, 1963). This visualizes a steady flow of people and ideas back and forth across Bering Strait, with little change in the way of life needed as long as they remain in this general area. However, once a group moves into a different ecological zone, change must occur if they are to survive. Ultimately a new cultural tradition adjusted to this environmental zone would develop and would spread relatively rapidly to the limits of the zone both through actual migration and cultural diffusion.

How might we characterize Arctic archaeology in 1962? Despite all the stepped-up activity, it is still the least-known and most understaffed area in North America. In contrast to the continental United States, where salvage archaeology is a major preoccupation and directive force, field work is almost entirely problem-oriented. Historic archaeology has taken only its first steps—e.g., VanStone's excavations at Taral (VanStone, 1955) and Hadleigh-West's work at the Sitka Fort. Prehistoric research is still very largely at the stage of preoccupation with chronology and sequence. Techniques and theory have been brought in almost entirely from outside, and there is perhaps more influence from the Old World in this realm than in many other parts of America. With few exceptions, work is carried on by outsiders, as in the early days of the Southwest or Meso-America. The role of the amateur archaeologist is virtually nonexistent, although the pothunter is a significant factor in Alaska—

especially a unique variety of the species, the aboriginal pothunter with a vested interest in his local sites. In Arctic Canada, on the other hand, protection and control have been exemplary. As to the state of knowledge, "there is much greater diversity in terms of distinctive cultures or cultural complexes than was previously known or even suspected." (Campbell, 1962, p. 442) "Unpredicted sites and cultures are turning up at a bewildering rate." (Giddings, 1962a, p. 155) We may well wonder if there is any other area where the picture changes so radically every few years. "Understandably, novel schemes must be devised to fit facts to theory." (Giddings, 1962a, p. 155) The result has been a number of differing interpretations of the current picture. There is realization that any such interpretation becomes obsolete almost immediately, but agreement on the usefulness of periodic attempts at overall synthesis. (Is any other area so well synthesized?) It is characteristic of all syntheses that they largely ignore southwestern Alaska—a fatal weakness if this should prove to be, as some suspect, the hearth and climax of Eskimo culture. Two excellent new relative sequences, the beaches of Cape Krusenstern and the stratified sites of the southern Yukon, now permit a much more accurate temporal positioning of widely scattered finds and also allow more precise reckoning of cultural relationships over a wide geographical area (Campbell, 1962, p. 442).

The data of archaeology, human biology, and linguistics from both sides of Bering Strait provide no evidence whatever of population movements from Asia to America in the last 5000 years, although cultural diffusion in either direction is obvious. Thus, for example, we can no longer explain away the Athabascans as recent arrivals. "It appears that Bering Strait has never been subject to wide-scale migrations of peoples from Asia to America such as would account for the diversity of culture, physique and language among American Indians, but that it has maintained from the distant past a locally modifying population and culture, based upon the combined food resources of the land and sea, and has served as a narrow conduit through which diffusion has freely vibrated in both directions at all times." (Giddings, 1952b, p. 102) The Bering Strait area is thus increasingly being viewed as a major cultural hearth rather than as simply a funnel for ideas and things originating somewhere else. Though diffusion has been brisk, none of the coastal assemblages seems to have originated elsewhere. People apparently tended to stay put and to stick to their own way of life, although they were in contact with one another. As examples, one can cite the limited distribution of the Old Bering Sea or Ipiutak cultures. "Regardless of the resemblance of its art styles to those of distant central Asia, Ipiutak culture has not turned up at any great distance from its type site." (Giddings, 1960, p. 129) Thus the autochthonous nature of Eskimo culture is being generally recognized; no longer are there the former efforts to see it as an Old World import. But in addition to the Bering Strait hearth, southwestern Alaska, so long ignored and little known, is now coming to the fore to claim a key role in this process.

On an earlier time level, Irving's (1962) review of the evidence shows that there is no proof or even likelihood that any of the recognizable preceramic traditions of northern North America is derived from a known Asian prototype. Nor is there any clear evidence in the artifacts for actual migration between the two continents after the initial peopling of the Americas—although certain traits may have diffused very widely. (The Old World parallels adduced by MacNeish are in discrete traits rather than complexes.)

Despite our greatly increased knowledge of north Eurasian archaeology, we are no nearer to a solution of the puzzle of Woodland pottery origins than we ever were—although Old World affinities for Alaskan ceramics are less problematical. Neither are we any nearer to an understanding of the exact mechanism of De Laguna's circumpacific culture drift, or to an explanation of the parallels and similarities which she pointed out—although there is great reluctance today to see the Aleutians as a bridge of any sort. And despite fifteen years of activity in the north, we still know next to nothing about the archaeology of the Northern Athabascans. Even though they represent half of the American Arctic as here defined, the origins and history of the people and their culture remain a mystery. And what we do know about the archaeology of their territory tells us nothing about them.

Finally, the Dorset culture, long an enigma, is now seen not as aberrant but as part of an Arctic continuum—as an Eskimo culture produced by people who were physically Eskimo and very probably linguistically Eskimo as well (see Hammerich, 1958, p. 641). One cannot help, however, being struck by the relative simplicity of the prehistoric picture in the eastern Arctic as compared with the incredible, burgeoning diversity of the west. Is this merely an illusion to be dispelled by further field work, or does it reflect more limited human occupation in the east and over a shorter period of time? Is it possible that the eastern Arctic was not suitable for occupancy until more recent times?

Now to venture a few predictions as to the future of Arctic archaeology. I would agree with MacNeish that a coherent, comprehensible picture of Arctic American prehistory is within the realm of possibility in the not too distant future, although it is evident that no simple theory of Eskimo origins can any longer account for the diverse cultural manifestations that have come to light in the North and the many more that will certainly be found. Key problems as yet unsolved include the origins of the Athabascans and their culture, the origins and history of the "microlithic" traditions, the transmittal of the Woodland pottery if in fact this did take place, coast-interior relationships in Eskimo history, and whether a real dichotomy ever existed in this respect; the validity and interrelationships of the various regional traditions currently recognized—particularly those between southwest Alaska and other Eskimos; clarification of the apparent continuum of cultural evolution in the eastern Arctic from Sarqaq to modern Eskimo; an understanding of the relationships between the inhabitants of the tundra, forest, and Plains from earliest times to the present, which should grow out of better knowledge of the ecological basis of the prehistoric Arctic cultures; and, of course, the time, place, and factors responsible for the formation of what we could consider as the Eskimo way of life.

In the approaches to such problems, I think we can predict a growing interest in process (now that the framework is getting established), and this will imply a major concern with environment, ecology, and the possible role of climatic changes. As elsewhere, there will be an increasing trend toward the interdisciplinary approach. The tendency of our problems to cluster increasingly about certain focal points will lead to emphasis on more detailed site investigations. Finally, the trend toward a broader frame of reference will continue, fostering greatly increased awareness and knowledge of prehistoric development in northern and eastern Eurasia.

New developments in the human biology of the Arctic are based both on genetic studies of living populations, especially with regard to blood types, and on the bony remains of older residents. Only the serological data have appeared in print to any extent. Emphasis has been upon the Eskimo. The Sadlermiut collection secured on Southampton Island in 1959 by the University of Wisconsin is one of the largest skeletal populations of Eskimos ever subjected to study. The osteology of the Northern Athabascans, on the other hand, is virtually unknown.

Current thinking stresses the polymorphy of the Eskimo-Aleut stock. There is no "typical" Eskimo; rather, there seems to have been a chain of related populations in western Alaska comprising eight or ten racial variants. The Ipiutak type is one such—a perfectly good, though different, Eskimo. The Paleo-Aleut and Paleo-Konyag types are comparable variants. The so-called "classic" eastern Eskimo is classic only through the historical accident of having been discovered and studied first. Migrations carried this type far and wide, hence it looms larger than it deserves to in our mental picture. It is representative neither of the majority of living Eskimos nor of the "oldest" or "purest" Eskimo stock. Finally, the phenomenon of brachycephalization has been demonstrated to have occurred over the course of time in the larger Eskimo populations; it is only the small groups that have remained dolichocephalic to the persent day. Such significant physical alterations are due in every case to internal change, not to external factors such as Indian admixture.

The sharp racial dichotomy between Indians and Eskimos—which has major historical implications—has been further demonstrated on the basis of blood groups, secretor factor, and hemogloblins, as well as the morphology of the living. For some reason, this information has been slow to take hold, and has not yet permeated the thinking of some of our leading scholars.

In the field of Arctic linguistics there has been a certain amount of recent field work, as yet unpublished, and very largely devoted to Athabascan and related groups. The only comprehensive, modern linquistic studies among the Western Eskimo and Aleut are the works of our Scandinavian colleagues, L. L. Hammerich and K.

Bergsland. The few surviving Eyak were subjected to investigation by Fang-kuei Li in 1952 and Robert Austerlitz in 1961. The former has ventured the tentative conclusion that while Eyak is definitely related to Athabascan, it cannot be considered as one of the Athabaskan languages. Two major projects recently launched are that of the Wycliffe Bible translators, affiliated with the Summer Institute of Linguistics, who have a number of husband-and-wife teams planted in communities from Angoon to St. Lawrence Island for a twelve- to fifteen-year stretch; and the work sponsored by the Language Department at the University of Alaska under M. E. Krauss with National Science Foundation support. Groups visited by the latter project include the Chugach, Konyag, Atna, Tanaina, and lower Yukon area. Austerlitz' field studies of Gilyak, carried out in northern Japan, should also be mentioned.

In addition to this linguistic field work there has been publication and/or reworking of data gathered earlier and often by others. Under this heading we should mention first the subject of glottochronology, since our Arctic area has received more than its share of attention in this respect. Not all of the work has escaped criticism, especially from our Scandinavian colleagues. (For an excellent review and critique of the subject, see Hymes, 1960.) It is of particular interest that the revised estimates now allow greater time depth for the Eskimo-Aleut divergence, ranging from 4600 to 6000 years, since this is in keeping with the latest archaeological evidence from the Aleutians, which would no longer support the previous 3000-year figure. The divergence of Yupik and Inupik is estimated at 1500–2000 years. Estimates for the Athabascan languages seem to fit the known picture, insofar as there is one; this includes divergence of Tlingit more than 2000 years ago. Curiously, the northern Athabascan languages diverge as much from one another as do the northern from the southern.

The subject of language relationships as such has received less attention. The most noteworthy development is that the common origin of Eskimo and Aleut, long doubted or rejected by many scholars, is now beyond question. This stock is now seen as composed of three separate languages—Yupik, Inupik, and Aleut—each with dialectical variations. As Hammerich rightly insists, "the problem of the origin of the Eskimo culture should not be separated from that of the origin of the Eskimo language." (1958, p. 644) Yet although Sapir as long ago as 1916 (1916, p. 82) postulated Alaska as the Eskimo hearth on the grounds that this best accorded with the linguistic evidence, the run of archaeologists and ethnologists have manifested little awareness or concern for such evidence during the ensuing forty-five years. It is still necessary to call attention to the point at the present day. Another suggestion traceable to Sapir is the possible relationship of Athabascan and Sino-Tibetan, which has more recently been considered by Shafer and by Swadesh.[5]

There has been a dearth of purely descriptive linguistics. We might mention under this rubric the volume of Kamchadal texts from Jochelson's manuscripts, published by Dean Worth (1961), with the promise of a dictionary in preparation. The previous neglect of this strategic, important, and fascinating group is at last being remedied.

In the field of mythology and folklore, a small number of short comparative or analytical studies have appeared since the war, but no major works. The most noteworthy are Margaret Lantis' analysis of Nunivak mythology for clues to personality (1953), and Ann Chowning's study of the Raven myths of northeastern Asia and northwestern North America (1962), which corrects the erroneous picture left by the work of the Jesup Expedition and has important historical implications.

Turning finally to ethnology, the postwar years seem to have brought a lull in field work—in marked contrast to the archaeological picture. They were marked, however, by the publication of a number of significant monographs based on previous field studies. Osgood's exhaustive study of Ingalik culture (1940, 1958, 1959) certainly ranks as one of the really important contributions, and displays more of a theoretical orientation than the rest, but is perhaps overburdened with methodology. It has been remarked that in sheer detail it has no rival since Boas' "Central Eskimo"; but there is little attempt at interpretation, and it has the inherent weakness of overdependence on a single informant. Honigmann's perceptive accounts of the Kaska (1949, 1954) also rank high, especially in the realms of social relations and personality, where on some topics he

[5] See *International Journal of American Linguistics*, 18, pp. 12–19 and 178–81; and 23, pp. 116–17.

provides the best data yet available on any Northern Athabascans. Also of high quality are Lantis' reports on Nunivak (e.g., 1946, 1959b), Rainey's study of Point Hope (1947), and McKennan's 1959 monograph on the Upper Tanana. Nor can we omit mention of Diamond Jenness' charming little volume of reminiscences of Arctic Alaska in 1913–1914 (Jenness, 1957). For the most part, these are studies of precontact culture. Despite the fact that the western Alaskan Eskimo comprise the bulk of all Eskimos and display the most highly developed culture and the greatest local variation, it is noteworthy that they continued to be largely ignored by anthropologists, in striking contrast to the intensive documentation available on the small, scattered populations of Arctic Canada and Greenland.

In the early 1950s, field work began to pick up. De Laguna's Tlingit project carried out ethnographic investigations at Angoon and Yakutat, and more recently among the Atna of the Copper River to round out coverage of contiguous groups. Coordinated studies were also conducted by Catharine McClellan in southern Yukon Territory. A major goal has been to examine the culture history of related peoples in quite different environments. Carpenter's sojourn among the Aivilik on Southampton Island has provided revealing insights into the nature of Aivilik art and the attitudes involved in the creative process, as well as the whole conceptual framework of experience (Carpenter, Vorley, and Flaherty, 1959). Spencer's ecologically oriented study at Point Barrow has resulted in a major monograph (1959) on the precontact culture of the North Alaskan Eskimo, that has been termed possibly the finest Eskimo ethnography ever published.

There have also been studies of a more topical nature. Noteworthy among these are Laughlin's (1952a) demonstration of the basic cultural unity of the Eskimo and Aleut—an important theoretical contribution; Lantis' monograph on Alaskan Eskimo ceremonialism (1947); her extensive paper on folk medicine (1959a); Marsh's analysis of Eskimo-Aleut religion (1954); Oswalt's paper on ethnobotany (1957); and Dorothy Ray's semipopular book on Alaskan ivory carving (1961).

In addition, the Arctic has, of course, had its share of the recently fashionable interest in culture and personality. In this category, Margaret Lantis has made probably the most important contribution to our knowledge of Alaskan Eskimo personality, with the publication of eighteen life stories which provide an inside view of Nunivak culture and explore Nunivak personality dynamics (1959b). Among the most active field workers should be mentioned Jane Hughes—whose investigations on St. Lawrence Island are not yet readily available—and Irma Honigmann, who has published some of her findings on the Kaska (Underwood and Honigmann, 1947) and Great Whale River Eskimo (Honigmann and Honigmann, 1953). Seymour Parker (1962) has made a significant contribution to the subject of the so-called "Arctic hysterias" in his consideration of the relationships between psychiatric symptoms and the sociocultural environment, with the aim of facilitating an understanding of why, when Eskimos become mentally ill, they are prone to manifest particular psychological symptoms. Along this same line, Wallace and Ackerman have outlined an interdisciplinary approach to the study of mental disorder among one highly restricted group, the Polar Eskimos (1960).

The ethnography of Siberian peoples also received some attention —e.g., Dorothy Libby's (1960) ethnohistoric studies on the Chukchi, and the writer's analysis of precontact Kamchadal culture (Chard, 1961).

Reviewing the developments of the past decade, we might say that they are characterized by the fading out of the trait-distribution orientation that was so dominant a feature of Arctic ethnology from 1917 to 1947; by an aversion, with a few honorable exceptions, to salvage ethnography—the rescue of rapidly vanishing cultures— especially in Canada; and by an overwhelming trend toward community studies (which have a certain inherent monotony) and applied anthropology. Among those interested in social organization there has been a flare-up of interest in the so-called "Eskimo" type of kinship system and social structure (e.g., Giddings 1952a, Hughes 1958), with the demonstration that all speakers of Eskimo do not practice Eskimo social organization—especially the Bering Sea groups—and that there is in fact no overall inclusive "Eskimo" pattern in such matters. Hughes, for instance, has proposed an explanation for the local development of clans on St. Lawrence Island. The subjects of polygamy and wife-lending also seem to exert a perennial fascination (e.g., Dunning 1962, Guemple 1961, Spencer 1958). But by and large, various aspects of culture change are the chief subjects of research today. This development is an outgrowth of the intensified contact situation of postwar years, the increase in population and in size of communities, and the rapidity with which the whole life of the Arctic people is changing. But the sudden and tremendous spurt of activity in the past few years is also due to new sources of support—first and foremost from the Canadian government. The bulk of this recent work is still unpublished. An outsider like the writer can say little on his own, and must depend almost entirely on information and views derived from colleagues active in the field.

Of the Alaskan community studies, only those of Hughes on St. Lawrence Island (1960) and VanStone on Point Hope (1962b) have appeared in final form. The former followed up an investigation by the Leightons fourteen years earlier, and hews to the thesis that disintegration is to be expected in situations of cultural change. Norman Chance has tested this thesis in his study of Kaktovik on the Arctic coast, with negative results (1960). VanStone's monograph, although in a sense following up Rainey's earlier work at Point Hope, is a functional and acculturational study of a contemporary community. Other community studies from the point of view of culture change include Berreman's visits to Nikolski (Umnak Island) in 1952 and 1962; the Honigmanns' intensive investigations in the triethnic settlement of Great Whale River on Hudson Bay (1952); June Helm on "Lynx Point," a Slave Indian settlement (1961); and many products of the Canadian boom of the past few years (e.g., investigations by Cohen and by VanStone on levels of acculturation in the Mackenzie Valley-Great Slave Lake area), some of which are already appearing in the new series published by the Northern Coordination and Research Center in Ottawa.

Some of this activity perhaps comes under the heading of applied anthropology. The leading role in Alaska here has been played by Margaret Lantis, operating through the Arctic Health Research Center. Her paper on Eskimo reindeer herding can be singled out in particular as one of the classic studies in applied anthropology (1952). She has also been particularly concerned with problems of

culture and health. VanStone and Oswalt have also made contributions in this genre, both in Alaska and more recently in Canada—
e.g., their studies of changing settlement and leadership patterns at
Eskimo Point among resettled Caribou Eskimo (Oswalt and Van-
Stone, 1960) or Oswalt's statement (1961) on guiding culture
change among Alaskan Eskimos. Again, much work remains unpublished as yet, and I have been able to mention only a small portion of
what has taken place in recent years.

What directions does ethnological work in the Arctic seem likely
to take in the near future? Present conditions of change in this area
suggest a number of topics that will attract interest. The increasing
involvement with the money economy raises problems of the meaning of money here, particularly as a symbolic device for controlling
the environment; at the same time the prevalent economic instabil-
ity adds a disturbing factor in the new patterns, with repercussions
in such areas as mental health. The trend toward concentration of
native populations in larger settlements leads to new subsistence
patterns as well as new social realignments. Such communities will
inevitably become foci of research attention, especially in Canada
where the shift from the previous very small groupings is most
striking and where there are many composite communities with no
aboriginal basis that offer special problems in interpersonal relations.
Another trend is the emergence of the nuclear family as the primary
socioeconomic unit—although the recent interest in Eskimo descent
and kinship groupings suggests that studies of the older systems
(of which we still know little) will continue to draw some attention. Development programs in the north are running into basic
problems of leadership, such as the disappointing record of community councils in many areas, that call for examination. In general,
we may expect the current boom in community studies to continue
as long as support is forthcoming; these will provide a certain
amount of ethnographic data as a by-product—hopefully, in little
known areas—and will bring forth a mass of material on all aspects
of culture change and acculturation. As social, cultural, and economic problems inevitably increase in the north in the wake of
present-day trends and activities, we may also predict that responsible agencies will turn increasingly to anthropologists for assistance
in dealing with them.

REFERENCES

Campbell, John M., editor (1962a). "Notes and News: Arctic," *American Antiquity*, 27, No. 3, pp. 442–46.

———(1962b). *Prehistoric Cultural Relations between the Arctic and Temperate Zones of North America.* Arctic Institute of North America, Technical Paper No. 11.

Carpenter, Edmund, Frederick Vorley, and Robert Flaherty (1959). *Eskimo.* Toronto, University of Toronto Press.

Chance, Norman A. (1960). "Culture Change and Integration: an Eskimo Example," *American Anthropologist*, 62, No. 6, pp. 1028–44.

Chard, Chester S. (1961). *Kamchadal Culture and Its Relationships in the Old and New Worlds.* Madison, University of Wisconsin Press.

Chowning, Ann (1962). "Raven Myths in Northwestern North America and Northeastern Asia," *Arctic Anthropology*, 1, No. 1, pp. 1–5. Madison.

Collins, Henry B. (1937). "Archeology of St. Lawrence Island, Alaska," *Smithsonian Miscellaneous Collections* 96, No. 1.

———(1955). "Archaeological Research in the North American Arctic," *Arctic Research*, pp. 184–94 (Arctic Institute of North America Special Publication No. 2).

———(1960). Comment on J. L. Giddings, "The Archeology of Bering Strait," *Current Anthropology*, 1, No. 2, pp. 131–36.

Cooper, John M. (1946). "The Culture of the Northeastern Indian Hunters: a Reconstructive Interpretation," in Frederick Johnson, ed., *Man in Northeastern North America*, pp. 272–305.

Damas, David (1963). *Igluligmiut Kinship and Local Groupings: A Structural Approach.* National Museum of Canada, Bulletin No. 196. Ottawa.

Davidson, Daniel Sutherland (1937). *Snowshoes.* Memoirs of the American Philosophical Society, 6. Philadelphia.

De Laguna, Frederica (1946). "The Importance of the Eskimo in Northeastern Archaeology," in Frederick Johnson, ed., *Man in Northeastern North America*, pp. 106–42.

———(1947). *The Prehistory of Northern North America as Seen from the Yukon.* Memoirs of the Society for American Archaeology, No. 3.

———(1956). *Chugach Prehistory. The Archaeology of Prince William Sound, Alaska.* Seattle, University of Washington Press.

———(1960). *The Story of a Tlingit Community: A Problem in the Relationship between Archeological, Ethnological and Historical*

Methods. Bureau of American Ethnology Bulletin 172. Washington.

De Laguna, Frederica, et al. (1964). *Archeology of the Yakutat Bay Area, Alaska.* Bureau of American Ethnology Bulletin No. 192. Washington.

Dunn, Stephen P. and Ethel (1963). "The Transformation of Economy and Culture in the Soviet North." *Arctic Anthropology,* 1, No. 2, pp. 1–28. Madison.

Dunning, R. W. (1962). "An Aspect of Recent Eskimo Polygyny and Wife Lending in the Eastern Arctic," *Human Organization,* 21, pp. 17–20.

Ford, James A. (1959). *Eskimo Prehistory in the Vicinity of Point Barrow, Alaska.* Anthropological Papers of the American Museum of Natural History, 47, Part 1. New York.

Fried, Jacob, editor (1964). "Contact Situations and Their Consequences in Arctic and Subarctic North America." *Arctic Anthropology,* 2, No. 2, pp. 1–60. Madison.

Giddings, J. L. (1952a). *The Arctic Woodland Culture of the Kobuk River.* Philadelphia, University Museum.

———(1952b). "Ancient Bering Strait and Population Spread," *Selected Papers of the Alaskan Science Conference,* pp. 85–102.

———(1952c). "Observations on the 'Eskimo Type' of Kinship and Social Structure," *Anthropological Papers of the University of Alaska,* 1, No. 1, pp. 5–10.

———(1960). "The Archeology of Bering Strait," *Current Anthropology,* 1, No. 2, pp. 121–30.

———(1962a). "Cultural Continuities of Eskimos," *American Antiquity,* 27, No. 2, pp. 155–73.

———(1962b). "Onion Portage and Other Flint Sites of the Kobuk River," *Arctic Anthropology,* 1, No. 1, pp. 6–27. Madison.

———(1964). *The Archaeology of Cape Denbigh.* Providence, Brown University Press.

Gubser, Nicholas J. (1965). *The Nunamiut Eskimos: Hunters of Caribou.* New Haven, Yale University Press.

Guemple, D. L. (1961). *Inuit Spouse-Exchange.* M. A. thesis duplicated by Department of Anthropology, University of Chicago.

Hadleigh-West, Frederick, editor (1963). "Early Man in the Western American Arctic. A Symposium." *Anthropological Papers of the University of Alaska,* 10, No. 2.

Hallowell, A. Irving (1926). "Bear Ceremonialism in the Northern Hemisphere," *American Anthropologist,* 28, No. 1, pp. 1–174.

Hammerich, L. L. (1958). "The Origin of the Eskimo," *Proceedings of* the 32nd *International Congress of Americanists*, pp. 640–44. Copenhagen.

Harp, Elmer (1961). *The Archaeology of the Lower and Middle Thelon, Northwest Territories.* Arctic Institute of North America, Technical Paper No. 8.

———(1964). *The Cultural Affinities of the Newfoundland Dorset Eskimo.* National Museum of Canada Bulletin 200. Ottawa.

Helm, June (1961). *The Lynx Point People: the Dynamics of a Northern Athapaskan Band.* National Museum of Canada Bulletin No. 176. Ottawa.

Honigmann, John J. (1949). *Culture and Ethos of Kaska Society.* Yale University Publications in Anthropology, No. 40. New Haven.

———(1952). "Intercultural Relations at Great Whale River," *American Anthropologist*, 54, No. 4, pp. 510–22.

———(1954). *The Kaska Indians: an Ethnographic Reconstruction.* Yale University Publications in Anthropology, No. 51. New Haven.

Honigmann, Irma, and John Honigmann (1953). "Child Rearing Patterns among the Great Whale River Eskimo," *Anthropological Papers of the University of Alaska*, 2, No. 1, pp. 31–50.

Hughes, Charles C. (1958). "An Eskimo Deviant from the "Eskimo" Type of Social Organization," *American Anthropologist*, 60, No. 6, pp. 1140–47.

———(1960). *An Eskimo Village in the Modern World.* Ithaca, Cornell University Press.

———(1965). "Under Four Flags: Recent Culture Change Among the Eskimos." *Current Anthropology*, 6, No. 1, pp. 3–69.

Hymes, D. H. (1960). "Lexicostatistics So Far," *Current Anthropology*, 1, No. 1, pp. 3–44.

Irving, William (1962). "A Provisional Comparison of Some Alaskan and Asian Stone Industries," *Arctic Institute of North America, Technical Paper*, No. 11, pp. 55–68.

Jenness, Diamond (1957). *Dawn in Arctic Alaska.* Minneapolis, University of Minnesota Press.

———(1962). *Eskimo Administration: I. Alaska.* Arctic Institute of North America, Technical Paper No. 10.

———(1964). *Eskimo Administration: II. Canada.* Arctic Institute of North America, Technical Paper No. 14.

———(1965). *Eskimo Administration: III. Labrador.* Arctic Institute of North America, Technical Paper No. 16.

Lantis, Margaret (1946). *Social Culture of the Nunivak Eskimo.* Transactions of the American Philosophical Society, 35, Part 2. Philadelphia,

———(1947). *Alaskan Eskimo Ceremonialism.* Monographs of the American Ethnological Society, No. 11. New York.

———(1952). "Eskimo Herdsmen," in E. Spicer, ed., *Human Problems for Technological Change*, pp. 127–48. New York, Russell Sage Foundation.

———(1953). "Nunivak Eskimo Personality as Revealed in the Mythology," *Anthropological Papers of the University of Alaska*, 2, No. 1, pp. 109–74.

———(1959a). "Folk Medicine and Hygiene: Lower Kuskokwim and Nunivak-Nelson Island Areas," *Anthropological Papers of the University of Alaska*, 8, No. 1, pp. 1–75.

———(1959b). *Eskimo Childhood and Interpersonal Relationships: Nunivak Biographies and Genealogies.* Seattle, University of Washington Press.

Larsen, Helge (1961). "Archaeology in the Arctic, 1935–60," *American Antiquity*, 27, No. 1, pp. 7–15.

Larsen, Helge, and Froelich Rainey (1948). *Ipiutak and the Arctic Whale Hunting Culture.* Anthropological Papers of the American Museum of Natural History, 42. New York.

Laughlin, W. S. (1952a). "The Aleut-Eskimo Community," *Anthropological Papers of the University of Alaska*, 1, No. 1, pp. 25–46.

———(1952b). "Contemporary Problems in the Anthropology of Southeastern Alaska," *Selected Papers of the Alaskan Science Conference*, pp. 66–84.

———(1963). "The Earliest Aleuts," *Anthropological Papers of the University of Alaska*, 10, No. 2, pp. 73–91.

Laughlin, W. S., and W. G. Reeder (1962). "Rationale for the Collaborative Investigation of Aleut-Konyag Prehistory and Ecology," *Arctic Anthropology*, 1, No. 1, pp. 104–8. Madison.

———(1966). "Studies in Aleutian-Kodiak Prehistory, Ecology and Anthropology." *Arctic Anthropology*, 3, No. 2. Madison.

Libby, Dorothy (1960). "Three Hundred Years of Chukchi Ethnic Identity," *Selected Papers of the Sixth International Congress of Anthropological and Ethnological Sciences*, pp. 298–304. Philadelphia.

McKennan, Robert A. (1959). *The Upper Tanana Indians.* Yale University Publications in Anthropology, No. 55. New Haven.

———(1965). *The Chandalar Kutchin.* Arctic Institute of North America, Technical Paper No. 17.

MacNeish, Richard S. (1959). "A Speculative Framework of Northern American Prehistory as of April 1959," *Anthropologica*, N.S., 1, pp. 7–23. Ottawa.

———(1963). "The Early Peopling of the New World—as Seen from the Southwestern Yukon," *Anthropological Papers of the University of Alaska,* 10. No. 2, pp. 93–106.

———(1964). *Investigations in Southwest Yukon: Archaeological Excavation, Comparisons and Speculations.* Papers of the Robert S. Peabody Foundation for Archaeology, 6, No. 2. Andover.

Marsh, Gordon H. (1954). "A Comparative Survey of Eskimo-Aleut Religion," *Anthropological Papers of the University of Alaska,* 3, No. 1, pp. 21–36.

Osgood, Cornelius (1940). *Ingalik Material Culture.* Yale University Publications in Anthropology, No. 22, New Haven.

———(1958). *Ingalik Social Culture.* Yale University Publications in Anthropology, No. 53. New Haven.

———(1959). *Ingalik Mental Culture.* Yale University Publications in Anthropology, No. 56. New Haven.

Oswalt, Wendell H. (1957). "A Western Eskimo Ethnobotany," *Anthropological Papers of the University of Alaska,* 6, No. 1, pp. 17–36.

———(1961). Guiding Culture Change among Alaskan Eskimos, *America Indigena,* 21, pp. 65–83, 151–70. Mexico.

———(1963). *Napaskiak: An Alaskan Eskimo Community.* Tucson, University of Arizona Press.

Oswalt, Wendell H., and James W. VanStone (1960). "The Future of the Caribou Eskimos," *Anthropologica,* N.S., 2, No. 2, pp. 154–76. Ottawa.

Parker, Seymour (1962). "Eskimo Psychopathology in the Context of Eskimo Personality and Culture," *American Anthropologist,* 64, No. 1, pp. 76–96.

Rainey, Froelich G. (1947). *The Whale Hunters of Tigara.* Anthropological Papers of the American Museum of Natural History, 41, No. 2, New York.

Rainey, Froelich, and Elizabeth Ralph (1959). "Radiocarbon Dating in the Arctic," *American Antiquity,* 24, No. 4, pp. 365–74.

Ray, Dorothy Jean (1961). *Artists of the Tundra and the Sea.* Seattle, University of Washington Press.

Sapir, Edward (1916). *Time Perspective in Aboriginal American Culture: A Study in Method.* Canada Department of Mines, Geological Survey, Memoir 90. Ottawa.

Spaulding, Albert C. (1946). "Northeastern Archaeology and General Trends in the Northern Forest Zone," in Frederick Johnson, ed., *Man in Northeastern North America,* Andover, Mass., Phillips Academy, pp. 143–67.

Spencer, Robert F. (1958). "Eskimo Polyandry and Social Organization,"

106   CHESTER S. CHARD

Proceedings of the 32nd International Congress of Americanists, pp. 539–44. Copenhagen.

———(1959). *The North Alaskan Eskimo: A Study in Ecology and Society*. Bureau of American Ethnology Bulletin 171. Washington.

Taylor, William E. (1959). "Review and Assessment of the Dorset Problem," *Anthropologica*, N.S., 1, pp. 24–46. Ottawa.

Underwood, Frances W., and Irma Honigmann (1947). "A Comparison of Socialization and Personality in Two Simple Societies," *American Anthropologist*, 49, No. 4, pp. 557–77.

VanStone, James W. (1955). "Exploring the Copper River Country," *Pacific Northwest Quarterly*, 46, No. 4, pp. 115–23.

———(1962a). "An Archaeological Collection from Somerset Island and Boothia Peninsula, N.W.T.," *Royal Ontario Museum, Art and Archaeology Division, Occasional Paper* 4, pp. 1–63. Toronto.

———(1962b). *Point Hope. An Eskimo Village in Transition*. Seattle, University of Washington Press.

———(1965). *The Changing Culture of the Snowdrift Chipewyan*. National Museum of Canada Bulletin No. 209. Ottawa.

Wallace, Anthony F. C., and Robert E. Ackerman (1960). "An Interdisciplinary Approach to Mental Disorder among the Polar Eskimos of Northeast Greenland," *Anthropologica*, N.S., 2, No. 2, pp. 249–60. Ottawa.

Worth, Dean Stoddard (1961). *Kamchadal Texts Collected by W. Jochelson*. 'S-Gravenhage, Mouton & Co.

FRED EGGAN

Northern Woodland Ethnology

THE GROWTH of our knowledge of Northern Woodland ethnology parallels on a smaller scale the development of American anthropology as a whole. For the purposes of the present survey I shall be concerned primarily with the Algonkian-speaking populations north of the Great Lakes–St. Lawrence region, although I will have something to say about their linguistic relatives and neighbors to the south and west.

This northern region has had a long and interesting history, dating from the voyages of Jacques Cartier in 1535, and has played an important role in the development of our continent, but our scientific knowledge of its aboriginal peoples and their cultures is much more recent. The central figure in our knowledge of the Northern Woodlands is Frank G. Speck. Speck began his pioneer researches among the Montagnais and Naskapi in 1908, and over the next two decades he literally put them and their neighbors on the ethnographic map. By 1926 he was able to present a survey and interpretation of "Culture Problems in Northeastern North America," which summed up what he had learned and set the stage for further research.

Here he was primarily concerned with historical problems—with the relations of the Northeastern Algonkians to their neighbors, and with the origins of Northeastern culture patterns and their relations to the circumpolar culture complexes constructed by Birket-Smith and Gudmund Hatt. Speck at this time saw the Northeast as "one of the world's marginal culture zones, an archaic one, where human groups have resided for a long time apart from cultural changes and innovations which have arisen elsewhere on the continent." (Speck, 1926, p. 272) But he raised the question of whether the cultural simplicity of the area was pristine, or arrived at through cultural reduction; and he touched on most of the problems which later were to be significant.

In the following two decades a number of Speck's students and associates at the University of Pennsylvania, notably A. I. Hallowell, D. S. Davidson, and Loren C. Eiseley, began field and library research on the Northern Woodlands, extending their activities over a wider geographical area and a greater range of problems. Joining them in this period were such scholars as Father John M. Cooper and Regina Flannery of Catholic University; Julius Lips, W. D. Strong, Diamond Jenness, Truman Michelson, W. J. Wintemberg, and Ruth Landes, among others. Speck's early observations on "The Family Hunting Band as the Basis of Algonkian Social Organization" (1915) were tested and broadened, and the aboriginality of the family hunting territory system was debated. But of greater significance were the new directions of research: a greater interest in problems of ecology, a more sophisticated approach to social structure, a new concern with processes of cultural change, a realization of the importance of archaeology and linguistics, and a growing awareness of the role of the individual in social interaction and the significance of personality structure for the understanding of culture process.

Several of these new directions converge in the work of Hallowell. Beginning with a survey of "Bear Ceremonialism in the Northern Hemisphere" (1926), he concentrated his attention during the decade of the 1930s on the Northern Ojibwa, or Salteaux, and spent most of his summers systematically investigating a series of related problems among the bands of the Lake Winnipeg–Berens River region. Here he was able to study the ecology of the family hunting system under neoaboriginal conditions, establish the significance of cross-cousin marriage as a social system, and unravel the psychological characteristics of the Northern Ojibwa with the aid of case studies and projective tests.

This period culminated with the symposium on "Man in Northeastern North America" (Johnson, 1946), held at Andover in December 1941, but not published until after the war. This volume, which was edited by Frederick Johnson and dedicated to Speck, is a landmark in American anthropology. It not only summarizes (in 300 pages) what had been accomplished in four decades of research, but outlines new problems for the future. Douglas Byers' survey of the environment of the Northeast is followed by five papers devoted to various aspects of the archaeology of the region by W. C. McKern, James B. Griffin, William A. Ritchie, Frederica de Laguna, and Albert C. Spaulding. W. W. Howells surveys the physical types of the Northeast, and Carl and Erminie Voegelin bring together the linguistic researches of Truman Michelson and Leonard Bloomfield. Hallowell discusses the psychological characteristics of the Northeastern Indians, and Margaret Fisher surveys the mythology of the region in relation to Algonkian mythology as a whole. The "descriptive survey" and "reconstructive interpretation" of the culture of the Northeastern Indians were prepared by Regina Flannery and John M. Cooper, respectively.

These discussions cast doubt on some of the earlier reconstructions of culture history in the Northern Woodlands. Father Cooper, in particular, critically reviews the hypotheses of his predecessors with regard to the origin and development of the Northeastern hunting culture and its accretions. He finds the evidence for the circumpolar "ice-hunting" and "snowshoe" stages insufficient, and proposes an ecologically conditioned "taiga economy" in its place. He also considers the family hunting ground system as representing a more recent local development in the Northeast, though he still believes it antedates white contact.

In the meantime Speck had begun to penetrate further into the inner world of the Northeastern Indians, and in *Naskapi, the Savage Hunters of the Labrador Peninsula* (1935), he presented their conceptions of religion and cosmology. Here his linguistic skills and his ability to create close personal relationships with Indian friends were important ingredients in his success. By an analysis of native terms he was able to discover a systematic relationship between their view of the universe, their conception of man's relation to nature, and the proper conduct of man in society. Here a functional viewpoint is to the fore; though Speck is still concerned with distributions, these are subordinated to the understanding that can come from context.

The present writer became interested in the Northern Algonkians about this same time, in connection with an attempt to understand some puzzling features in the kinship systems of the Cheyenne,

Arapaho, and Gros Ventre (Eggan, 1937). A few years earlier Hallowell had asked, "Was Cross-Cousin Marriage Formerly Practiced by the North-Central Algonkian?" (1928), on the basis of his study of kinship terms in early dictionaries. The question was answered in the affirmative by W. D. Strong, who had just returned from Northern Labrador where he found cross-cousin marriage in full operation among one of the bands of northern Naskapi (Strong, 1929). During the next few years the practice was reported by a number of investigators from several Northern Woodland groups. Hallowell's account of "Cross-Cousin Marriage in the Lake Winnipeg Area" (1937) outlined the characteristics of the resulting social system, and proposed the hypothesis that variations in Northern Algonkian kinship systems are "intelligible as a result of acculturative processes and differences in local conditions." (ibid., p. 108) At about the same time Ruth Landes was carrying out a series of studies of the Ojibwa of southern Canada, and her comprehensive account of social organization on the Rainy Lake reserve (Landes, 1937) provided some important differences. In the postwar period the application of Hallowell's working hypothesis has proved remarkably productive in furthering our understanding of change in social systems.

In a region such as the Northern Woodlands, occupied by populations who depended primarily on hunting, fishing, and gathering for their subsistence, the environmental characteristics are obviously of great importance. In the early days of American anthropology, in reaction to extreme conceptions of environmental determinism, the environment was considered as an essentially neutral factor in cultural development. It sets limits but it was not a creative force. Speck accepted this view, to begin with, but his early interest in natural history, which led him to study the family hunting territory system, soon took him beyond into the religious beliefs concerning nature and the animal species. He also influenced several students in these directions, notably D. S. Davidson, Loren C. Eiseley, and A. I. Hallowell.

Davidson's detailed studies of the Grand Lake Victoria and Tête de Boule bands (Davidson, 1926, 1928) showed important variations in social organization which suggested environmental determinants. These and other studies (Davidson, 1937) led to a greater concern

for the ecological characteristics of winter life, and to a consideration of the significance of migratory and sedentary characteristics in
the game animals on which the Northern Woodland populations
depended. Speck and Eiseley accepted these considerations as valid
in a paper on the "Significance of Hunting Territory Systems of the
Algonkian in Social Theory" (1939), but were more concerned
with the attack by Diamond Jenness (1935) on the aboriginality of
the family hunting territory system.

One of my own students, Arch Cooper, investigated the "Ecological Aspects of the Family Hunting Territory System of the Northeastern Algonkians" (1942) in a Master's thesis, and suggested that
the variations could best be explained in ecological terms. He found
both a sociological and an ecological gradient from northeast to
southwest within the area, and developed a model to explain their
interrelationships in terms of five factors: (1) the productivity of the
natural environment, (2) the definiteness of the local organization,
(3) the degree of band cohesion, (4) the strength of patriliny, and
(5) the relative frequency of elementary and extended family units.
Hallowell (1949) also devoted attention to these problems, and has
discussed "The Size of Algonkian Hunting Territories, A Function
of Ecological Adjustment," utilizing his own field data from the
Berens River region. Here he is relatively unconcerned with the
question of the aboriginality of the system, but concentrates his
attention on the specific conditions which control the variables of
size and composition of the winter hunting groups, the size of the
hunting tracts, and the rules governing their transfer.

The question of the aboriginality of the family hunting territory
system of the Northeastern Algonkians has led to considerable controversy in the literature. Jenness, on the basis of his study of the
Parry Island Ojibwa, had come to the conclusion that their system
had developed since the advent of the fur trade, and that this conclusion might be applied to the Eastern Algonkians in general (1935,
pp. 4–6). Julian Steward supported this position, on the basis of the
intimate functional relationship of the family ownership system to
the highly specialized economy introduced by the fur trade (1936,
p. 339), and his own studies of the Athabascan-speaking Carrier of
British Columbia. Since the documentary data in the *Jesuit Relations*
could be interpreted either way, there was no adequate solution

until Eleanor Leacock carried out field research among the Montagnais-Naskapi in 1950, centered on this specific problem. Her
monograph on *The Montagnais "Hunting Territory" and the Fur
Trade* (1954) clarifies the issues and comes to the conclusion that
the family hunting territory is post-Columbian and definitely related to the fur trade in the area of southeastern Labrador. She also
analyzes the dynamics of band and family composition in terms of
modern acculturative forces—the fur trade, the trading post, and
European settlement—and sees the same processes at work among
other Arctic hunters. Her concluding sentences (p. 43) are worth
quoting because they signalize a postwar point of view:

"Acculturation" is now recognized as encompassing more than the
final breakdown of Indian societies. . . . It is becoming increasingly evident that Indian tribal life as recorded in the nineteenth and even late
eighteenth centuries reflected important changes which had already come
about as a result of the Indians taking an active part in the worldwide
growth of trade and commerce. . . . The present study has taken the
position that the northern Algonkians are no exception. Their apparent
primitivity is deceptive. In order to reconstruct their aboriginal culture,
one cannot simply record their recent life and subtract those traits that
are of obvious European origin. One must work from an understanding
that fundamental socio-economic changes have been taking place in
some parts of their area for over three hundred years, one aspect of
which is the development of the family hunting territory.

Hallowell has extended our knowledge in a different direction
through his emphasis on the individual and his psychological characteristics. From his researches during the decade of the 1930s have
come a remarkable series of papers which the Philadelphia Anthropological Society has recently published under the title *Culture and
Experience* (1955). While his ultimate aim is to formulate the necessary and sufficient conditions that make human existence possible, he
has also analyzed the characteristics of the Ojibwa world as it is
conceptualized and experienced by the individual, and has tenta-
tively formulated the psychological character structure of the Eastern Woodland Indians. Here he has built in part on the foundation
furnished by Speck, but through his utilization of projective techniques and case histories he has been able to penetrate considerably
further.

Hallowell's and Landes' studies of the Northern Ojibwa have stimulated a number of studies of the Southern Ojibwa or Chippewa in Minnesota and Wisconsin, who have had a somewhat different recent history and have been subject to a greater degree of reservation acculturation. Barnouw, in a study of *Acculturation and Personality among the Wisconsin Chippewa* (1950), emphasized the atomistic nature of their social structure and attempted to explain it in terms of a persistence of aboriginal patterns, reinforced by the partial maintenance of personality structure through child training and other procedures. This analysis, based on documentary data, field reports, and life history materials, has been supported by Ernestine Friedl (1956) and challenged by Bernard James (1961) and Harold Hickerson (1960). In his reply to the latter, Barnouw (1961) clarifies his position but continues to maintain his view that "social atomism" is an old Chippewa pattern.

In the light of Hallowell's accounts of the Northern Ojibwa, and R. W. Dunning's recent monograph (1959) on the same region, it is clear that Ruth Landes' characterization of Northern Ojibwa society as "atomistic" is not tenable in any terms but comparative ones. The further data provided by Hickerson in his recent monograph on *The Southwestern Chippewa, an Ethnohistorical Study* (1962) would seem to dispose of the concept of "social atomism," so far as the Southern Ojibwa are concerned. It is probable that the social isolation noted by Barnouw and others is a product of reservation life. Here Hallowell's observations on the Lac du Flambeau Ojibwa of Wisconsin (1955, Chapters 18 and 19) are pertinent. Comparing their personality structures as seen through the Rorschach data with those of the Berens River and Lake Winnipeg region, he finds a continuity of basic psychological pattern, but emphasizes that important modifications in their psychological structure have taken place.

It is at Flambeau where we can see reflected in the Rorschach data an introversive personality structure being pushed to the limits of its functional adequacy. The whole trend is one that seems to be accelerating in a regressive direction. These people are being thrown back on their psychological heels, as it were. They are compelled to function with a great paucity of inner resources. There is a kind of frustration of maturity. [Hallowell, *ibid.*, pp. 351-52]

He goes on to point out that a large percentage of the subjects at Flambeau fall into the "poorly adjusted" category and suggests that there are factors at work which set barriers to the achievement of personal adjustment, particularly the absence of any positive substitute for the aboriginal value system based on religious belief (*ibid.*, p. 357). It seems probable that the Wisconsin Chippewa have arrived at their present social and psychological condition largely through deculturation under modern reservation conditions.

The present writer returned to the problem of cross-cousin marriage in the postwar period and surveyed the new data available from the Northern Algonkian groups in terms of Hallowell's hypothesis noted earlier (Eggan, 1955). It seems clear that cross-cousin marriage had been the basis for the social structure of the northern groups, and that a clan system had been added later among the Ojibwa. The series of changes in kinship and marriage, which Strong documented for the Naskapi, were largely the result of mission influence on the more southern bands, and it is highly probable that Catholic teaching is responsible for the obsolescence of cross-cousin marriage among the Montagnais nearer the St. Lawrence. But the series of shifts among the Northern and Southern Ojibwa, and in the Plains groups, must have a different explanation. Here the structural requirements of a wider integration incident to life in a more favorable environment, and constant warfare, have been significant factors in the decline of cross-cousin marriage.

Harold Hickerson has made an important contribution to this problem in his recent study of the Southwestern Chippewa (1962). He traces these groups from their earlier residence at Sault Ste. Marie to the south shore of Lake Superior (where they lived from 1679–1765), and west into northern Minnesota and Wisconsin. Here they came into continued conflict with the Eastern Dakota, or Sioux, and Hickerson has documented the ecological basis of their warfare and its effects upon social and cultural life. One important result of warfare was that the village came to be the basic unit of social life, and the bands subordinate. For purposes of successful conflict against the larger Dakota villages, the Chippewa villages developed alliances and warrior organizations which were unknown in the north. Hickerson has found no reference to cross-cousin marriage for the southwestern Chippewa in the historic period. He concludes that they "had long since dropped the practice of bilateral cross-cousin marriage, not through influences attributable to simple acculturative factors but for dynamic sociopolitical reasons." (*ibid.*, p. 86)

A study titled "Central Algonkian Social Organization" (1958) by Charles Callender clarifies and documents this situation from a different standpoint. In analyzing the kinship systems and social structures of the various Algonkian-speaking tribes south of the Great Lakes, Callender enlisted the aid of Charles Hockett (1964), who was able to reconstruct enough kinship terms to demonstrate the presence of cross-cousin marriage among the proto-Central Algonkian populations. Callender attributes the loss of cross-cousin marriage to such factors as larger populations incident to agriculture, corporate clan groups, complex village organization, and warfare.

At the other end of the Ojibwa continuum, Dunning (1959) has made the first detailed study of the structure and functioning of a band organization throughout its yearly cycle and in relation to the new influences from the outside world. The Pekangekum band, among whom he worked in 1954–1955, is the most isolated of the Berens River bands studied by Hallowell two decades earlier. Here we have a detailed account of the ecology and economy, the summer and winter groupings, and the patterns of marriage and kinship. Of particular importance are the changes since the war, where government subsidies have brought the small residential units in from the trap-lines and drawn them to the trading post. With the growth of population the band becomes more endogamous, and cross-cousin marriage begins to shift from close to more distant relatives.

A. L. Kroeber, some time ago (1939, p. 35), noted that the Ojibwa were among the least known of American tribes, despite the number of scholars who had studied them. It is clear from the above remarks that we now have most of the ingredients for a detailed and comparative account. The dissemination of the Ojibwa from a residence in the vicinity of Lakes Huron and Superior both northwest and southwest during the seventeenth and eighteenth centuries is well attested. The differences between the Berens River bands and the Minnesota and Wisconsin villages, let alone those of the Plains Ojibwa, indicate what can happen to society and culture within a relatively short time. The Northern Ojibwa (Saulteaux) under neoaboriginal conditions reduced the size of their bands and spread their hunting-trapping units over wide but defined territories. Cross-cousin marriage shifted from a preferential to a prescriptive pattern, and the kinship terminology was modified accordingly. The totemic clan system was reduced in scope and significance, and the ritual system was simplified. Warfare was absent. The Southern Ojibwa, on the other hand, with greater economic resources, increased their population density, and the village and its institutions became the basic social unit. The winter hunting bands were subordinate to the village community, and the patrilineal clans may have developed additional ritual functions. The Midewiwin became a village or even intervillage institution. The narrow but intensive integration brought about by cross-cousin marriage was no longer adequate in the south, where loyalties and alliances were on a village level. And the century of continuous conflict with the Dakota over hunting grounds made survival depend upon matching the efficiency of the foe. If personality remained the same under these differences, it must be largely independent of society and culture.

The differences between the Northern and Southern Ojibwa can be clarified both by studying the intermediate groups along the border and by examining the neighboring Cree to the north and the Central Algonkians to the south. The Cree, in a severer environment, have most of the institutions of the Northern Ojibwa—except for the clan system. The Central Algonkian tribes have elaborated the clan and phratry system as corporate groups, and have developed village-wide leadership and institutions. There is no trace of cross-cousin marriage in the kinship system; the latter has shifted to an Omaha type consonant with the lineage organization and clan exogamy.

From the little knowledge we have of the Eastern and Southeastern Algonkian groups south of the St. Lawrence and along the eastern seaboard, it is probable that similar processes were at work. The Wabanaki, according to Speck (1926), showed radical changes in political life, social organization, and mythology as a result of contacts with the Iroquois and other groups to the south. A detailed comparison with the Southern Ojibwa might show many interesting parallels. The Southeastern Algonkians had a still more complex sociopolitical organization as a result of interaction with the Cherokee and other tribes of the Southeast, but we have few details of their organization and cultural life.

We have so far outlined some of the major developments in Northern Woodland ethnology, and it is time to say a few words about future prospects. There are a number of recent developments which will affect the future directions of research in the Northern Woodlands, as well as a number of problems which would repay intensive research, now that we have more sophisticated conceptual tools and greater resources.

In an earlier survey of "The Ethnological Cultures and their Archeological Backgrounds" (Eggan, 1952) in the Eastern United States, I emphasized the important role which archaeology was beginning to play in the reconstruction of the culture history of that region. George I. Quimby's recent account of *Indian Life in the Upper Great Lakes, 11,000 B.C. to A.D. 1800* (1960) presents an outline of the new knowledge gained from geology, paleontology, archaeology, palynology, and radiocarbon dating, of the prehistory of this important region. While the glaciers began their retreat about 11,000 B.C., the ice lasted north of the Superior basin until about 4500 B.C., according to Quimby, which effectively prevented the establishment of plants and animals, as well as human populations, until a later period. Since Hudson Bay is assumed to be the last continental center of glaciation, it is probable that the Labrador peninsula was covered for an even longer period.

These data suggest that Speck's view of the Northeast as a refuge area for "archaic" populations retaining earlier culture patterns is no longer tenable, even with the modifications suggested by Father Cooper. But there is evidence of the northward spread of early man as the ice retreated or melted, and as vegetation and animals took its place. Quimby identifies and dates a series of archaeological assemblages in the Great Lakes region, beginning with Paleo-Indian hunters, Archaic Boreal Indians, the Old Copper culture, and Early, Middle, and Late Woodland groups, some of the latter being ancestral to historic tribes.

In the Northeast the archaeological sequences are not yet clear. Here the Eskimo Dorset culture has a number of elements which resemble Indian types, but the age of its earliest manifestations is not known. I have not been able to keep abreast of archaeological research in New England and the Maritime Provinces, though these are obviously of great potential importance.

The utilization of historical sources and documentary data has long been an important research technique with regard to the Eastern Woodlands generally. John M. Swanton in the Southeast and Speck and his students in the East and Northeast have made masterly use of these materials to delineate aboriginal and early historic culture patterns. But in recent years there has been an increasing tendency to utilize such materials for studies of social and cultural change. An important early study along these lines is F. M. Keesing's monograph, *The Menomini Indians of Wisconsin* (1939), which he subtitled "A Study of Three Centuries of Cultural Contact and Change." Vernon Kinietz' *The Indians of the Western Great Lakes, 1615–1760* (1940) presents the ethnographic data available in the documentary sources on five tribal groups, but without further interpretation.

The establishment of the National Archives and the passage of the Indian Claims Act have led to renewed research in the post-war period on specific questions but have also resulted in a number of important by-products. The rapprochement which is taking place between historians and ethnologists is one important event, signalized by the formation of the American Indian Ethnohistoric Conference and the publication of the journal *Ethnohistory*. Another is the establishment of archival collections on the Indian populations of particular regions, such as the archives of the Great Lakes–Ohio Valley Research Project at Indiana University. From such collections it is now possible to write an almost year-by-year account of many Indian groups, as well as to clarify and extend our knowledge of particular problems. Harold Hickerson's ethnohistorical account of the Southwestern Chippewa (1962) and Anthony Wallace's "Political Organization and Land Tenure among Northeastern Indians, 1600–1830" (1957), are examples of what we may expect in the immediate future. In the longer run we can look forward to a more sophisticated history of the American Indian, in which the cultural component will have adequate representation.

The potentialities of linguistics for the unraveling of ethnological problems has not as yet been systematically applied to the Northern Woodland regions. Through the pioneer researches of Bloomfield and Michelson we have considerable information on the Central Algonkian languages, but their subgroupings and relations to Western and Eastern branches are not yet clear. Here lexicostatistics should be of assistance in clarifying relationships and subgroupings. That Cree-Montagnais-Naskapi are dialects of one language, and Ojibwa-Ottawa-Salteaux-Algonkian another, from the standpoint of the linguist, has not been sufficiently taken into account in ethnological comparisons and interpretations. Nor have the possibilities of reconstruction of cultural traits through linguistic comparison been carried very far.

At the other extreme, Mary Haas' recent demonstration (1958) that the Algonkian and Gulf language stocks are genetically related presents us with new perspectives. When coupled with earlier suggestions by Sapir and others, they suggest an ultimate genetic unity for most of the languages in Eastern North America, omitting the Eskimo and Athabascans. This linguistic unity may make Kroeber's classification of the Eastern and Northern Woodlands as variants of a single major culture area more intelligible, and may give us greater control over the interpretation of the archaeological record.

The time now seems ripe, also, for anthropologists to return to some of the classic problems of the Northern Woodlands with sharper concepts and better controls. Totemism is one such classic problem, and the term "totem" itself is an Ojibwa word. While American anthropologists, notably A. A. Goldenweiser, attempted to analyze totemism out of existence, it is still very much alive. Even though the Central Algonkian varieties may not be of classical type, they are still highly relevant to the problems of man's relation to nature. Speck's characterization of hunting as a "sacred" activity suggests one important approach.

Another series of problems lies in the field of religion. The Midewiwin ritual, for example, is now ready for intensive study, both in terms of its historical development and in comparison with similar rituals elsewhere in the region. It has long been asserted to be post-Columbian, but the evidence has not yet been assembled in detail. The so-called *windigo* or *witiiko* psychosis, found mainly among the Cree and Northern Ojibwa, is now under study by psychiatrists with interesting results (i.e., Parker, 1960). But they have analyzed the problem primarily from the standpoint of the victim, largely ignoring the belief patterns of the society. Dunning (1959, opposite p. 83) was able to get drawings of the *windigo* cannibal spirit from eleven- and twelve-year-old boys, but no older person would draw or discuss this spirit. Such "repression," if it is repression, should warrant investigation, along with the role these beliefs may play in Northern Woodland groups. Their absence from Eskimo and Northern Athabascan society is intriguing in this connection.

Last, but by no means least, we come to the study of modern Indian communities in their own terms. Acculturation studies are relatively recent in American anthropology, but a number are already under way in the Northern Woodlands, or recently completed. We have noted the pioneer study of the Menomini by Keesing published just before the war. This formed the basis for a more sophisticated study of the processes in Menomini acculturation by George and Louise Spindler, who divided the Menomini into five acculturative categories and studied the sociocultural and psychological aspects of change among both men and women (G. Spindler, 1955; L. Spindler, 1962). Sydney Slotkin's study of Menomini Peyotism (1952) in terms of its social and cultural role in reservation life, is also important in this connection.

A broader and longer term study is the "Algonkian project" of the Ethnology Section of the National Museum of Canada under the direction of Tom McFeat. Much of the early support for ethnological research in the Northeast originally came from museums, including the University Museum in Philadelphia, but after 1930 museums had limited resources for research and devoted much of their attention to displays and housekeeping. During the last few years, however, there are signs of a renaissance, led by ethnologists such as William Fenton, Donald Collier, John C. Ewers, and others. It is quite fitting, therefore, to find that Tom McFeat is proposing to utilize the resources of the National Museum for a systematic and long-term study—or restudy—of the various Algonkian groups in the Northeast, beginning with the Montagnais-Naskapi and the

Micmac and Malecite, and extending to the Cree and Ojibwa. Mc-Feat has given us a preliminary survey of the proposals in "Museum Ethnology and the Algonkian Project" (1962).

The first objective of the study is to describe the stability and changes in group structure over the last hundred years, utilizing previous studies as a baseline. Here the ethnologists can often start with Speck's early data on band composition and territorial arrangements, and follow the changes down to the present. They distinguish two major types of groupings: "territorial" groups who are still hunters and trappers, and "reserve" groups who are usually employed for wages and who generally live on the government reserves.

For these groups they plan to investigate such questions as knowledge of the environment, space orientations, change in band structure, shifts in territorial arrangements, expressions of aggression, public opinion and values, problems of leadership, the character of the shifts from "territorial" to "reserve" groups, and relations with the White world. Some sixteen students and associates are currently at work on various phases of this project, so there should be a rapid accumulation of comparable data.

A comparison of this project with the original objectives of Frank Speck as he began his researches on the Montagnais some fifty years ago gives us an indication of how far anthropology has come in half a century. But it also reminds us of the continuity of anthropology, in that the data collected by these pioneers and the insights they had into Northern Woodland life are still valid and useful. They add a dimension to our data which we would not otherwise have, and furnish a baseline against which to measure stability and change. We can also see that anthropology progresses by asking new questions, as well as on occasion returning to the old ones for a fresh look.

REFERENCES

Barnouw, Victor (1950). *Acculturation and Personality among the Wisconsin Chippewa*. American Anthropological Association, *Memoir* 72.
———(1961). "Chippewa Social Atomism," *American Anthropologist*, 63, pp. 1006–1013.

Callender, Charles (1958). *Central Algonkian Social Organization.* Publications of the Milwaukee Public Museum, No. 7.

Cooper, Arch (1942). *Ecological Aspects of the Family Hunting Territory System of the Northeastern Algonkians.* Master's thesis, University of Chicago.

Davidson, D. S. (1926). "Family Hunting Territories of the Grand Lake Victoria Indians," *22nd International Congress of Americanists,* pp. 69–96.

——(1928). "Notes on Tête de Boule Ethnology," *American Anthropologist,* 30, pp. 18–46.

——(1937). "Snowshoes," American Philosophical Society, *Memoir 6.*

Dunning, R. W. (1959). *Social and Economic Change among the Northern Ojibwa* (Toronto, University of Toronto Press).

Eggan, Fred (1937). "The Cheyenne and Arapaho Kinship System," in Fred Eggan, ed., *Social Anthropology of North American Tribes,* pp. 35–95 (Chicago, University of Chicago Press), pp. 35–95.

——(1952). "The Ethnological Cultures and their Archeological Backgrounds," in J. B. Griffin, ed., *Archeology of the Eastern United States* (Chicago, University of Chicago Press, 1952), pp. 35–45.

——(1955). "Social Anthropology: Methods and Results," in Fred Eggan, ed., *Social Anthropology of North American Tribes,* rev. ed. (Chicago, University of Chicago Press), pp. 519–48.

Friedl, Ernestine (1956). "Persistence in Chippewa Culture and Personality," *American Anthropologist,* 58, pp. 814–25.

Griffin, J. B. (ed.) (1952). *Archeology of the Eastern United States* (Chicago, University of Chicago Press).

Haas, Mary (1958). "A New Linguistic Relationship in North America: Algonkian and Gulf Languages," *Southwestern Journal of Anthropology,* 14, pp. 231–64.

Hallowell, A. I. (1926). "Bear Ceremonialism in the Northern Hemisphere," *American Anthropologist,* 28, pp. 1–175.

——(1928). "Was Cross-Cousin Marriage Formerly Practiced by the North-Central Algonkian?" *23rd International Congress of Americanists,* pp. 519–44.

——(1937). "Cross-Cousin Marriage in the Lake Winnipeg Area," *Publications of the Philadelphia Anthropological Society,* 1, pp. 95–110.

——(1949). "The Size of Algonkian Hunting Territories, A Function of Ecological Adjustment," *American Anthropologist,* 51, pp. 35–45.

——(1955). *Culture and Experience* (Philadelphia, University of Pennsylvania Press).

Hickerson, Harold (1960). "The Feast of the Dead among the Seventeenth Century Algonkians of the Upper Great Lakes," *American Anthropologist*, 62, pp. 81–107.

——(1962). *The Southwestern Chippewa, an Ethnohistorical Study.* American Anthropological Association, *Memoir* 92.

Hockett, Charles (1964). The Proto-Central Algonkian Kinship System," in Ward H. Goodenough, ed., *Explorations in Cultural Anthropology* (New York, McGraw-Hill), pp. 239–57.

James, Bernard (1961). "Social-Psychological Dimensions of Ojibwa Acculturation," *American Anthropologist*, 63, pp. 721–46.

Jenness, Diamond (1935). *The Ojibwa of Parry Sound.* Anthropological Series 17, National Museum of Canada, *Bulletin* 78.

Johnson, Frederick (ed.) (1946). *Man in Northeastern North America.* Papers of the Robert S. Peabody Foundation for Archaeology, 3. Andover, Mass.

Keesing, F. M. (1939). *The Menomini Indians of Wisconsin.* American Philosophical Society, *Memoir* 10.

Kinietz, Vernon (1940). *The Indians of the Western Great Lakes, 1615–1760.* Occasional Contributions from the Museum of Anthropology of the University of Michigan, 10.

Kroeber, A. L. (1939). *Cultural and Natural Areas of Native North America.* University of California Publications in American Archaeology and Ethnology, 38.

Landes, Ruth (1937). *Ojibwa Sociology.* Columbia University Publications in Anthropology, 29.

Leacock, Eleanor (1954). *The Montagnais "Hunting Territory" and the Fur Trade.* American Anthropological Association, *Memoir* 78.

McFeat, Tom (1962). *Museum Ethnology and the Algonkian Project.* National Museum of Canada, Ottawa, *Anthropological Papers*, 2.

Parker, Seymour (1960). "The Wittiko Psychosis in the Context of Ojibwa Personality," *American Anthropologist*, 62, pp. 603–23.

Quimby, George I. (1960). *Indian Life in the Upper Great Lakes, 11,000 B.C. to A.D. 1800* (Chicago, University of Chicago Press).

Slotkin, Sydney (1952). *Menomini Peyotism.* American Philosophical Society, *Memoir* 74.

Speck, Frank G. (1915). "The Family Hunting Band as the Basis of Algonkian Social Organization," *American Anthropologist*, 17, pp. 289–305.

——(1926). "Culture Problems in Northeastern North America," American Philosophical Society, *Proceedings*, 65, pp. 272–311.

124 FRED EGGAN

———(1935). *Naskapi, Savage Hunters of the Labrador Peninsula.* (Norman, Okla., University of Oklahoma Press.)

Speck, Frank G., and Loren C. Eiseley (1939). "Significance of Hunting Territory Systems of the Algonkian in Social Theory," *American Anthropologist*, 41, pp. 269–80.

Spindler, George (1955). *Sociocultural and Psychological Processes in Menomini Acculturation.* University of California Publications in Culture and Society, 5.

Spindler, Louise (1962). *Menomini Women and Culture Change.* American Anthropological Association, *Memoir* 91.

Strong, W. D. (1929). "Cross-Cousin Marriage and the Culture of the Northeast Algonkian," *American Anthropologist*, 31, pp. 277–88.

Steward, Julian (1936). "The Economic and Social Basis of Primitive Bands," in R. H. Lowie, ed., *Essays in Anthropology Presented to A. L. Kroeber*, (Berkeley, University of California Press), pp. 331–50.

Wallace, Anthony (1957). "Political Organization and Land Tenure among Northeastern Indians, 1600–1830," *Southwestern Journal of Anthropology*, 13, pp. 301–21.

WALLACE L. CHAFE

A Challenge for Linguistics Today

THE scientific and social revolution now taking place everywhere in the world will have as one of its inevitable consequences the obliteration of much of the raw material of linguistics. I believe it is a safe guess that within just the next few generations more than half of the 4,000 or so languages in the world will pass out of existence. This is a staggering loss. The linguistic diversity which has existed on earth for countless millennia, and which probably until recently increased with increasing numbers of men, is rapidly shrinking to a not too distant point where it is conceivable that the number of the world's languages will not very greatly exceed the number of members in the United Nations.

To make this situation more concrete, let me illustrate it with some details from North America. The course of linguistic attrition in South America, Africa, Asia, and elsewhere is of course different in some respects, particularly in regard to the amount of time that will be involved, but the influences at work are similar and the ultimate consequences will be everywhere comparable.

There were probably something more than three hundred languages in America north of Mexico at the beginning of the sixteenth century. Roughly half of them survive today. Well over half of these in turn are no longer spoken by children and thus cannot last much beyond the end of this century. Of the remainder, the most viable are languages like Navaho, Ojibwa, Cree, and Eskimo, still spoken by tens of thousands of people, still insulated to at least some extent from the dominant languages of the United States and Canada, and still being transmitted to children in some areas. Nevertheless I believe that no one seriously doubts that these languages too are doomed, and that only a few additional generations will see them as dead as the others. I will hazard the guess that Canadian French will sooner or later share the same fate, and more certainly so those Old World languages without governmental support now spoken by large and small groups of Americans and Canadians. If one could be here to collect, it might not be foolish to bet that barring major social upheavals English will become the only indigenous language north of the Rio Grande before the year 2100.

Let me narrow down the focus even further, and in so doing point to what linguists have done and are doing about this situation in a representative group of American languages.

The Indian language with which I am most familiar is Seneca, spoken by a couple of thousand people in New York State and Ontario. It virtually ceased being transmitted to children several decades ago, and there is, I believe, hardly anyone now under thirty years of age who speaks the language fluently. Probably the twentieth century is the last in which any satisfactory record of it can be made. So far a morphology and several specialized texts have been published and a dictionary is nearing completion (Hewitt, 1903, pp. 221–54; 1918; pp. 715–43, 756–90; Chafe, 1960–61; 1961). Together these things provide what we may regard as the minimum desirable description of any language. Much further work could be done on phonology, syntax, semantic patterns, dialect variation, ethnolinguistics, psycholinguistics, and so on.

Closely related to Seneca are the other Northern Iroquoian languages: Cayuga, Onondaga, Oneida, Mohawk, Tuscarora, and Huron. Their life expectancies are no better, and for some worse, than that of Seneca. Varying amounts of field work have been done on each of these languages within recent times, but the only modern publication outside of a few texts (Hewitt, 1903; 1928; Barbeau, 1960) is a description of Oneida verb morphology (Lounsbury, 1953). Whatever else has been collected remains in manuscript.

The value of unpublished material as a permanent record of a language varies greatly with the nature of the material and with the collector. It is sometimes nearly impossible for other individuals to use, and sometimes quite broadly usable. It is, however, never as valuable a record as a published work, not only because of the infinitely greater accessibility of the latter but also, and of equal importance, because to prepare material for publication involves an ordering of it that only its collector can accomplish. A linguistic field worker inevitably learns much about a language that does not appear in his undigested notes, and it is only he who possesses the digestive faculties necessary to turn these notes into a finished description. If he doesn't do it, we are left with archives full of material half-chewed.

Huron can be cited as a language which typifies the state of some others today and of many more in the future. There are two or three people alive now who spoke it well when they were young. Out of contact with each other, probably none of them has conversed in it for thirty years. The amount of forgetting that takes place over such a time is considerable, and seems strongest in the voluntary recall of vocabulary. It is interesting in contrast that the phonology seems well retained, that articulations seem not to have suffered much from disuse. Work with Huron informants today might produce a fairly adequate phonological description, a much attenuated grammar, and a lexicon of only shadowy proportions. We are fortunate that fuller material was collected by an ethnologist fifty years ago, and that he is now preparing it for publication. Hopefully it will be supplemented with tape recordings while there is still time.

The southern cousin of these languages is Cherokee, presently spoken by about 10,000 people, most of them in Oklahoma. There are still children who are learning it in some localities, although their number is continually diminishing. Unquestionably Cherokee will outlive the other Iroquois languages, probably by several generations. It is an especially interesting language, not only because of the relatively large number of speakers and their distinctive culture and history, not only because of its significance for comparative Iroquoian studies, not only because of its clear-cut differentiation into half a dozen localized dialects, but also because it is the only language indigenous to North America that has a written literature which has sprung from inside the culture itself.

In spite of the continuing and conspicuous presence of this provocative linguistic situation in our own back yard, American linguists have virtually ignored it. There is no satisfactory Cherokee grammar, no dictionary, and the only published text of any proportions was collected years ago by an ethnologist and prepared for publication by a visiting Belgian (Mooney and Olbrechts, 1932).

The only published discussion of Cherokee grammar was prepared at the University of Pennsylvania (Reyburn, 1953–54), but it is incomplete and restricted to the North Carolina dialect. No linguist has paid the slightest attention to Cherokee dialectology, although a brief visit in the company of a sophisticated Cherokee observer led me to believe that bundles of isoglosses are almost palpable across the eastern Oklahoma countryside.

The ability to read Cherokee will disappear long before the ability to speak it; it is, in fact, nearly gone now. If nothing is done to salvage their contents within just a few years, the large number of Cherokee documents now in various archives and in private hands will become considerably more difficult and often impossible to interpret. If we wait too long we may one day have to approach Cherokee writing as we now approach cuneiform tablets. In any case it is clear that written texts cannot be entirely equated with the spoken language through simple transliteration, that there are habits acquired in learning to read and write Cherokee which are distinct from speaking habits, and that these particular habits will pass out of existence very soon.

The older speakers of some Indian languages assert that young people nowadays no longer speak as they should, even when they speak at all. One infers from such remarks that there is a kind of young people's dialect which is an imperfect reflection of the proper speech of days past. There has been no systematic investigation of this question, but from brief work with a young speaker of Cherokee I believe that the notion is not unfounded so far as that language is concerned. There is, for example, a markedly reduced vocabulary, an avoidance of dual forms in favor of the plural, and an abandoning of inclusive prefixes in favor of the exclusive. Probably such peculiarities can be attributed to the transfer of habits from English, and also to the rapidly decreasing range of situations in which young people may be called upon to use Cherokee. A comparable situation is familiar among German immigrants' children who know only the verb forms with *du*. Thus, even while Cherokee may be around for many years to come, it may gradually become a distorted echo of the Cherokee that once was.

One of the major objectives of studying these languages is to be able to compare them and draw inferences concerning their history.

In undertaking such comparisons one becomes most painfully aware of the value of comprehensive published descriptions. Dictionaries are of course of first importance. In the case I am discussing, except for a few poorly recorded vocabularies there is absolutely no published dictionary now available for any Iroquoian language. While there is hope that this situation will shortly be remedied for Seneca and Huron, there is no immediate prospect that it will be remedied for the others. The result is that in order to find cognate forms it is necessary to search through old and unreliable sources with minimal hope of satisfaction, to write to the individuals who might have the needed material in their notes, or to visit a reservation in person. It is obvious that no very extensive comparative studies can be carried on in this fashion. There is no substitute for detailed, readily available dictionaries in depth. As Henry Hoenigswald has pointed out recently in print, "the kind of minimum information which is often the first (and occasionally remains for a long time the only) fruit of fieldwork, while it is likely to be quite adequately geared to the central needs of descriptive work, rarely contains all that the historian wants . . ." (Hoenigswald, 1962, p. 211).

So long as this situation holds, we will be unable to reconstruct very fully the history of the Iroquoian family, and we will be unable to test and expand the general theories of historical linguistics as they might be tested and expanded in this group of languages. In addition, we will be unable solidly to confirm or conscientiously to doubt those remote relations to language families which some linguists have been so eager to propose and which most anthropologists have been so eager to accept. This problem, as it concerns the Iroquoian family, has a long history. In 1845 the Englishman Robert Latham declared on the basis of vocabularies then available that, in effect, the Iroquoian, Caddoan, Siouan, and Muskogean families were all remotely related (Latham, 1846, p. 44). The first three of these families were included by Sapir in the larger Hokan-Siouan grouping in 1929, and Iroquoian and Caddoan were there suggested as forming a subgroup within that larger stock (Sapir, 1929). This hypothesized special relationship between Iroquoian and Caddoan has since then been widely accepted. No data to support it has ever been published, however—a fact which is not surprising since the Caddoan languages have been virtually unknown. Sapir's suggestion was, I believe, based largely on data from Pawnee. A brief text and grammatical sketch of that language appeared in 1936 (Weltfish, 1936), but it was certainly not enough to establish a relationship to Iroquoian. Since then there has appeared only a tentative discussion of Wichita phonemes (Garvin, 1950). I have myself been working on Caddo for several years, and there is room for hope that the other extant Caddoan languages—Pawnee, Arikara, and Wichita— may be comprehensively described while there is yet time. From my own experience I can say that the proposed relationship to Iroquoian, if it exists, is indeed remote, and that it will take extensive and detailed information from both families to validate it.

I have gone into this much detail on Iroquoian studies and their significance because I believe that the situation I have described is fairly typical of many language families throughout the world. Everywhere we can find languages slowly or rapidly disappearing, many of them superficially recorded with no immediate prospect of an adequate published description, and particularly no prospect of a dictionary. The thinness of descriptions hinders comparative work nearly everywhere. Nearly everywhere, too, there are proposed remote relationships among language families which can only be accepted on faith until these other deficiencies are overcome.

My desire here has been to emphasize the urgency of the situation which confronts linguists now, for while there is general agreement on the desirability of descriptive work there seems to be less appreciation of the fact that for such an overwhelming proportion of languages time is running out. And contrary to our experience with Latin and Greek, unwritten languages, once they are gone, are gone. They do not survive in bits and pieces as other cultural patterns often do for a surprisingly long time. A language is spoken by one generation, a handful of words and phrases are remembered as curiosities by the next, and then there is nothing. Nor can we quickly stuff a language like a passenger pigeon and have at least a good part of it always before us. Satisfactory recording takes months or years of dedicated work, work that provides thrills of discovery fully as exciting as those open to explorers in any field. But it is exploration with a deadline. And every discovery that is missed is a greater or lesser tragedy for linguistics and for the science of man.

REFERENCES

Barbeau, C. Marius (1960). *Huron-Wyandot Traditional Narratives in Translations and Native Texts*. National Museum of Canada *Bulletin* 165.

Chafe, Wallace L. (1960–61). *Seneca Morphology*. *International Journal of American Linguistics*, Vols. 26–27.

———(1961). *Seneca Thanksgiving Rituals*. Bureau of American Ethnology *Bulletin* 183.

Garvin, Paul L. (1950). "Wichita I: Phonemics," *International Journal of American Linguistics*, 16, pp. 179–84.

Hewitt, J. N. B. (1903). "Iroquoian Cosmology," 1st Part, Bureau of American Ethnology *Bulletin* 21, pp. 127–339.

———(1918). "Seneca Fiction, Legends, and Myths," Bureau of American Ethnology *Bulletin* 32, pp. 493–813.

———(1928). "Iroquoian Cosmology," 2nd Part, Bureau of American Ethnology *Bulletin* 43, p. 449–819.

Hoenigswald, Henry M. (1962). "Review of C. F. and F. M. Voegelin and Kenneth L. Hale, *Typological and Comparative Grammar of Uto-Aztecan*." *International Journal of American Linguistics*, 28 pp. 210–13.

Latham, Robert G. (1846). "Miscellaneous Contributions to the Ethnography of North America." *Proceedings* of the Philological Society for 1844–45 and 1845–46, pp. 31–50. London.

Lounsbury, Floyd G. (1953). *Oneida Verb Morphology*. Yale University Publications in Anthropology No. 48.

Mooney, James, and Franz M. Olbrechts (1932). *The Swimmer Manuscript*. Bureau of American Ethnology *Bulletin* 99.

Reyburn, William D. (1953–54). *Cherokee Verb Morphology*. *International Journal of American Linguistics*, Vols. 19–20.

Sapir, Edward (1929). "Central and North American Languages." In David G. Mandelbaum, ed., *Selected Writings of Edward Sapir* (Berkeley and Los Angeles, University of California Press, 1951), pp. 169–78.

Weltfish, Gene (1936). "The Vision Story of Fox-Boy, a South Band Pawnee Text," *International Journal of American Linguistics*, 9, pp. 44–75.

FREDERICK J. DOCKSTADER

Anthropology and the Museum

THE STORY of the development of American anthropology has been closely linked with Philadelphia from the time it could be considered a formal discipline. As previous papers have indicated, however, until recently the term *anthropology* essentially referred to the study of man's physical and biological being, and in the early days probably very few of those interested in the subject would have had any conception of the form which it takes today.

Thus, the early growth of museums was more primarily concerned with natural history, and it is not surprising that the collections were stronger in the fields of stuffed animals, geology, and flora and fauna from exotic areas, than in anthropological specimens. Nevertheless, it seems certain that even the earliest museums of which we have record included some material culture objects from other regions. Whether these should be more accurately considered in the realm of history is an argument which need not detain us here.

The museums movement has had its greatest strength in the United States, and I think it is fair to say that, with all respect to the great institutions in Britain and in Europe, the concept of the museum as a public institution, preserving and exhibiting man's works for the present and future generations, has had a unique development in this country. These institutions which we enjoy today and take for granted as part of our heritage, have for the most part grown out of the early private cabinets of curiosities which encompassed almost the whole range of human knowledge.

Most wealthy individuals had such what-not shelves, whose contents are fascinating even today. The range of knick-knacks knew no limits: natural history, archaeology, ethnology, geology, and "relics," were arranged cheek-by-jowl with little regard to order.

Their primary purpose was largely to amuse and astonish; and most of these accumulations were admittedly casually formed. Traveler's souvenirs or looter's treasure troves—they were all too often the mute evidence of cultural vandalism. It is truly remarkable that from such disorganized catchalls have come some of the great educational institutions of which we are justifiably so proud today.

More than one claimant has been put forth as the earliest formal museum in the United States. That honor is usually given to the Charleston Museum of South Carolina, which opened its doors in 1773. But more to our present interest is the beginning of anthropological museums. In this connection it is interesting to note that the distinction of being the first apparently belongs to Philadelphia, where Pierre Du Simitière established his American Museum on Arch Street in 1782, just nine years after the Charleston Museum opened. Although it only lasted for two years, its catalog, still extant, shows a strong ethnological content. Of those museums still in active operation, Dartmouth College in 1783 opened a formal museum and among its collections was a large number of carefully catalogued ethnological and archaeological treasures.

Almost immediately after this came a number of college and semi-public museums. During this period many of the educational institutions saw in the formation of such cabinets a means whereby student interest could be stimulated, donors flattered (and money thereby pried out of them), and a receptacle provided for the storage of those odds and ends which alumni were sending back from their travels. There was little formal museology employed; they were housed in glass-fronted cabinets or bookcases, with handwritten labels which bore varying degrees of enlightening information. The custodian was usually one of the faculty, and the manner in which the collections were maintained depended completely upon his devotion to this responsibility.

This pattern was characteristic through the middle of the nineteenth century, and there are few examples of a more formally established anthropological museum prior to about the time of the Civil War. One other development early in the 1800s had a strong influence, and this was the rise of the profit-making institution. Many individuals who traveled throughout the world brought back souvenirs of their travels. Among them were businessmen, adventurers, seamen, and a large number of artists. These people, for varying reasons, established museums (perhaps more properly called side shows) which were available to the public for a nominal admission charge, with the hope that a profit would result. In some instances these heterogeneous exhibits did manage to pay their way, but by and large most of them were not financially successful. One would suspect that a major cause for the failure of these early efforts was that they came at the wrong time, both financially and socially.

The artists mentioned above were forerunners of a group who have been more active in the establishment and healthy development of museums than perhaps any other, with the possible exception of the man of commerce seeking an outlet for his philanthropy or proudly supporting his community. Such men as the three Peales and Catlin, to mention only the better known, attempted to further their fortunes (or at least encourage an interest in their artistic efforts) by exhibiting the materials which they had gathered as props. And in 1818 William Clark established his Indian Museum in St. Louis, displaying many of the specimens gathered during his exploration with Meriwether Lewis. This was the first specialized American Indian museum in the world.

Eventually all of these early private collections open to the public were destroyed by fire, were sold on the auction block, or disappeared into the oblivion which has swallowed up so much of America's cultural heritage.

But it is of particular interest to note that Philadelphia saw the rise and fall of several museums, most notably the Peale, which in its heyday must have been an exciting place to visit. It would be a wonderful treat for us today to be able to turn time back a century and a half and look on some of the objects then displayed casually as simple, everyday utensils or implements. Merely to read the catalogs of the collections owned by Charles Wilson Peale, Du Simitière, or George Catlin makes the contemporary anthropologist weep at the thought of lost treasures.

But each of these has left something of its existence to us; in the University Museum, for example, are some of the remnants of these magnificent early collections, some even bearing their more or less adequate documentation—and it is just the ability to establish such a record of long continuity that makes the several institutions in this city so remarkable. In assaying the value and longevity of institutions of this nature, we often fail to give due consideration and credit to those individuals who, though rarely in the limelight, quietly treasure and protect specimens, data, and other materials in their care and are responsible for such continuity as we may enjoy today. May their number increase!

I would suspect that at first there was no real sense of competition between the college cabinets and the private exhibit galleries we have just discussed. In the first place, the goals of the two were completely separate, and the methods whereby each achieved its individual end were so disparate that probably the thought of competition did not arise. Moreover, the colleges of that day were private institutions, and the cabinets, if they existed at all, were essentially available only to students and most certainly would not be the sort of thing that the casual passer-by would drop in to inspect. As a matter of fact, I am rather doubtful that these cabinets enjoyed any considerable degree of visitor interest, since it would seem they had their greatest value and activity when the custodian made them available to the occasional visitor as something of a special honor.

Historically, the period up to 1850 represented the very gradual development of an institutional form which eventually came to be the public museum. More and more private individuals were forming collections, most of which stayed secluded within homes, but the idea of establishing a true educational institution which would serve the general public and, most particularly, the world of education, probably began with the gift of John Smithson in 1826 of a fortune for an "establishment for the increase and diffusion of knowledge." No will has ever been so fully executed. With the transferral in 1847 under the terms of this will of the large ethnological collections from the United States Patent Office to the future United States National Museum, the great period of the American museums was just ahead. True, in 1840 the Academy of Natural Sciences Museum was built, in 1843 the New York State Museum at Albany had just established its collections with the Louis Henry Morgan material, and Amherst in 1846 had built the first college museum building; nevertheless, most of the larger anthropological museums were founded between 1850 and 1900.

This era of major museum development was dominated by many of the great names in anthropology. Men like Powell, Hodge, Dorsey, and Uhle were sent out to bring back treasure to fill the then empty halls. Others like Putnam, Holmes, Dixon, and Mason labored to turn these collections into intelligible exhibits and useful teaching materials. The degree to which these collections were well rounded depended entirely upon the individuals responsible for the field work. That they are by and large so thoroughly representative of the various regions visited is testimony to the high caliber of the scientist-collectors.

Many of these projects were grandiose to an extreme. Some were intelligently thought out, as for example the efforts at the University Museum to present Near Eastern archaeology in well-balanced fashion following the work in Babylon and Sumer. But others were of the nature espoused by Squier, who suggested that one of the islands in the Hudson River be set aside for the restoration and reconstruction of the temple of Palenque. At this distant time it is amusing to note that although Squier's vision never came into being, the contemporary surge of interest in primitive art has almost succeeded in accomplishing his goal, albeit by a somewhat different avenue.

But to return. The greatest influences on museums and anthropological collections were undoubtedly the two great expositions of the late 1800s. The first, the Philadelphia Centennial in 1876, not only resulted in the later strength of the University Museum, but also in the establishment of several museums in this city, notably the Philadelphia Fine Arts Museum. The second, the World's Columbian Exposition in 1893, saw the birth of the Field Museum in Chicago. The great collections which were brought together for this purpose—and the displays designed for installation therein—had tremendous impact throughout the country. And just before the close of the century there was the National Export Exposition, which saw the founding of the Commercial Museum, an institution of astonishing ethnological wealth. Most of its accessions were selected by knowledgeable people as being representative of the arts and crafts of many then colonial areas. Much of this material was left at the Exposition, to avoid the costs of transportation back to the point of origin. We should count ourselves fortunate indeed that the values of 1900 were vastly different from primitive art values today!

With the exception of technical facilities which have become available to us, there have been few major changes in the general approach to museum exhibition since the time of Holmes, Putnam, and Mason. The classic culture-area concept of Mason still holds true, with minor modifications; the use of dioramas and sculptural groups perfected by Holmes has not been surpassed, and the scholarly integrity of Putnam continues to challenge museum exhibit men.

One other name should be brought into focus, that of Daniel Brinton, for this Philadelphia scholar exerted a major influence upon the maturing of the University Museum. A great Iroquois student, Brinton laid the groundwork upon which his successors have built a magnificent institution.

By 1900, then, a majority of the outstanding present-day anthropological museums had come into being, their programs were well formulated, and they had already established sound records of scholarship. Most of them were east of the Mississippi; the westward movement had not yet grown to a place where museums were yet possible. Teaching was one of the major duties of museum curators, and while some of the larger universities had just begun to grant anthropological degrees—Clark was first, in 1892, with a Ph.D. to Chamberlain, albeit in the Sociology Department—the major figures in the discipline were museum men, or had taken their training under museum circumstances.

About this time museums dedicated to special fields of interest became more numerous, with the appearance of such institutions as Wistar Institute, the Oriental Institute, the Museum of the American Indian, and others in the anthropological field.

With increased interest in anthropology developing in the universities, the rise of the social sciences, and the trend toward social consciousness, a gradual but steady flow began in which the teaching of anthropology became transferred from museums to university departments. Usually this was incorporated into the then existing sociology departments, and this continues to be true in all-too-many schools. With this change in direction came a change in emphasis. The newer faculties were less likely to be museum men, and were more and more scholars who had gained their experience by means of books rather than through the use of artifacts. The next fifty years were to see a trend toward orientation in the direction of social interrelationships rather than interest in material culture. The disappearance of many of the indigenous groups was partially responsible for this change, even though there are still many civilizations more or less aboriginal in form.

This shift has had a serious effect upon museums, since they cannot collect, preserve, and display the intangibles which the contemporary scholar finds of major interest. They likewise feel frustrated in realizing that much of the material in their collections suffers for want of study, and yet there is a great lack of scholars capable of such study. I think it is fair to say that an unfortunately large proportion of the people who have worked with Indian tribes are not able to handle adequately the material culture collections from that same tribe. To a museum curator this is a serious problem, for it means that he has no one to turn to for first-hand experience and information.

No mention has thus far been made of one of the great institutions in this city, and this deliberately so. The American Philosophical Society demands a section to itself, since it occupies a unique role in our story. From the time when Benjamin Franklin established the Junto in 1727 up to the present, this organization has enjoyed a particularly exciting role in American scholarship. In any consideration of museums or archives its merit increases, since it had at one time a fine collection and still maintains one of the great libraries of the world, housing rich manuscript collections of anthropological data, and a rich stock of documentary work on the American Indian. It has been in the forefront of the granting of funds for field work and for publications in the field of anthropology, and is indeed an institution in which Philadelphia as well as the entire country can take tremendous pride.

Just as Du Simitière brought forth on Arch Street one of the early collections of Indian material, the University on Spruce Street has represented another great wealth of anthropological research collections. From the time the first field expeditions to the Near East, Latin America, and the Orient brought back great bodies of varying materials, to the establishment of these in storage and in exhibit cases, the museum has served both the scholar and the lay visitor with equal responsibility. How many present-day students of anthropology have gotten their start here at the University Museum is impossible to say. No director knows the true influence of his institution; the child who comes in with an arrowhead for identification may, in later years, come to be one of the great names in archaeology, and it is this exciting possibility which makes working with youngsters so full of promise and so satisfying.

Thus, as the university more and more took the place of the museum in teaching anthropology, the museum turned to a different audience and, in this case, the general public benefited. Up until approximately 1930, most funds for field work and general exploration came from museums and were paid for by wealthy donors, whose names were emblazoned on the collections. With the rise of the great philanthropic foundations much of this changed; monies for expeditions became available through them, private donors' funds went to schools and to medical needs, and museums found themselves less able to attract large sums of money to do the necessary work. They thus had to turn to the public for support, and in so doing the emphasis in their exhibits had to change. No longer were the visual storage techniques satisfactory; the fact that one could see in a single case all of the types of arrowheads meant nothing to the visitor who simply wanted to know what an arrowhead was and how it was made.

Thus the past quarter-century has seen a remarkable change in museum exhibition techniques. One need only go into any of the halls of this institution to see the remarkable effects made possible by the development of new techniques of display, new lighting facilities, and by the imagination of the display artist. In such a change this region has kept pace. One of the finest archaeological collections or its type can be seen locally at the Carnegie Museum in Pittsburgh. Here the whole story of an archaeological sequence can be understood and immediately grasped, regardless of the lack of formal training of the viewer. The new halls here in the University

Museum present the trend toward the new look in museum work. Shortly a completely new museum complex, housing the great collections of the State, will open at Harrisburg, where John Witthoft and Fred Kinsey are busily preparing plans for the displays.

And what of this new look? What has it done to museums and perhaps to the general public? It is perhaps too early to judge completely, since, as with all developments of this nature, there are many good things and many bad things. On the good side, I think, would be the greater interest in museums as places where anyone may go and leave with a certain degree of understanding and profit. There is less of the bewilderment and confusion than was formerly the case, and it is certainly fair to say that the presentations do a greater degree of justice to the objects than in earlier days. At their best they are a magnificent experience which can only inspire the viewer to learn more; and even at their worst they are a satisfactory visual entertainment.

On the negative side is the fact that many of them fail to give well-rounded presentations, since they represent a high degree of selectivity and thus, in anthropological terms, result in a poorly balanced picture. It is also true that in most exhibits rarity takes precedence over commonness; it is not often that the curator dispassionately considers whether the object is rare because few have survived, or that it is rare because it was a freak in its own day and thus does not represent truly the culture in which it developed. An exhibit of esthetic freaks is not anthropology.

This whole problem of the presentation of the "great object" completely out of its anthropological context has become most particularly serious with the rise of interest in primitive art. There is certainly no reason why balance cannot be accomplished in such a field. Primitive art is certainly as respectable as Renaissance art, or numismatics, or any of a hundred other specially delimited studies. Unfortunately, in the particular instance we are discussing today, one of the greatest problems the contemporary museum man must face in the consideration of primitive art is this tendency to withdraw objects from their cultural context and ascribe to them completely foreign qualities, often resulting in that peculiar dichotomy which has confused art history students for the past decade. As a wry comment, it has been just as difficult for the primitive art student to define what he is about as for the present-day anthropologist to decide whether or not he is working in the social sciences.

One other concern in the contemporary remodeling of museum exhibits results from the practice of displaying smaller quantities of material. While much preferable to the older visible storage exhibits, it means the engorging of storage facilities. Sad to relate, rarely have I seen a plan developed in which facilities for study collections are increased in proportion to the remodeling accomplished in the exhibition halls. Since most museums start out on a renovation program with storage capacity already full, the retirement of a large body of material from the exhibits has meant cramming more and more into storage. Unless the need to accommodate this excess is taken into account in the original planning, it can only result in the eventual loss of a certain amount of the collections through attrition. It is fairly safe to say that much of the material presently in museum collections will not be available for any useful purpose in another twenty-five to fifty years. It is probably true that some of this can well be discarded, but the disposal of such material should be left to the curator, rather than to the impartial action of Father Time.

Today we are at a point where museums are enjoying a greater public response than ever before; there is probably not a single museum in the country which attracts fewer people than in previous years. Yet, at the same time, there is serious doubt about the degree to which their services are being most wisely used by scholars. This is certainly true in anthropology, and I suspect it is not very different in the other sciences. Unless and until university faculties realize that a student who studies anthropology without access to material culture is like a chemistry student who has never been in a laboratory, the museum will not fill its proper role.

Entertaining and educating the lay public is not enough; we have too great an investment in our collections, our abilities, and our knowledge to allow this to happen. And museums are not on the defensive, for their functions are too solidly balanced and too well understood not to be able to command this utilization; a signal example of this is the fact that art students, engineers, and medical researchers, to name but a few, have found unexpected dividends in museum collections.

At the risk of belaboring a point, I would like to draw a picture of anthropology one hundred years hence. There will be few, if any, aboriginal tribes—so the ethnologist will have no field work to look to. The archaeologist will find himself hard put to locate sites not covered with concrete or asphalt. Since everyone will probably speak a common tongue, the linguist will find himself severely restricted. The "one world" which we apparently demand will radically alter the work of the sociologist. The last physical anthropologist will have long ago succumbed to complete confusion. Only the psychiatrist will be on a twenty-four hour schedule.

This oversimplification is only to make a point: the anthropologist may well find himself facing the only research facility left open to him—the museum storage. How will he find it? Will the cupboard be bare?

And even more serious in that distant period is the simple fact that it is only by means of the material culture in museum collections that your children and mine will be able to gain any experience in depth of the indigenous peoples of the world, and the cultural developments which they painfully created. Books and pictures can give only part of the story.

It is this trust which has made the anthropological museums of the country the great cultural repositories they are today. And it is this feeling of concern for curious students a century hence which has caused these museum people to work together so effectively to build the institutions which are so important in Philadelphia today.

Contributors

WALLACE L. CHAFE received a doctorate in linguistics from Yale in 1958. Now a member of the Department of Linguistics at the University of California at Berkeley, Dr. Chafe has maintained an interest in American Indian languages with special work in the languages of the Seneca and Caddo.

CHESTER S. CHARD received his doctorate in anthropology from the University of California in 1953. He is now Professor of Anthropology, and he was formerly chairman of the Department of Anthropology at the University of Wisconsin. He is editor of *Arctic Anthropology*. With field work on Southampton Island in the Canadian Arctic, on the Alaska Peninsula, and in northern Japan, his major research interests are in the prehistory and culture history of northeastern Asia and its relationship with northern North America.

FREDERICK J. DOCKSTADER is Director of the Museum of the American Indian, Heye Foundation, which he joined in 1955. He has been, since 1958, Chairman of the Indian Arts and Crafts Board of the U. S. Department of the Interior. A Doctor of Philosophy from Western Reserve University in 1951, he has published *The Kachina and the White Man, Indian Art in America, Indian Art in Middle America,* and *Indian Art in South America.*

FRED EGGAN, now Harold H. Swift Distinguished Service Professor of Anthropology at the University of Chicago, received his doctorate from that University in 1933 and has been associated with the Department of Anthropology there for all of his academic life. He has done extensive field work with American Indian groups and in the Philippines. His special interests in anthropology have been in the areas of social anthropology and acculturation.

GORDON F. EKHOLM is Curator of Anthropology at the American Museum of Natural History. Dr. Ekholm received his Ph.D. in Anthropology from Harvard University in 1941, and he has been associated with the American Museum of Natural History since 1937. His interests have centered on the archaeology of Mexico and Central America.

JOHN F. FREEMAN received his doctorate in American Civilization from Harvard in 1960 with a biography of Henry Rowe Schoolcraft as his dissertation topic. From then until his sudden death in 1965, his major research interests were in the history of American anthropology, particularly during its formative years in the late eighteenth and early nineteenth centuries. His last teaching position was Assistant Professor of History at Kansas State University.

A. IRVING HALLOWELL, Emeritus Professor of Anthropology at the University of Pennsylvania, received his doctorate from that institution in 1924. He has been President of the American Anthropological Association and received the Viking Fund Medal and award in general anthropology in 1955. Although his interests cover the whole of the culture of the American Indians, he has made significant contributions in the field of personality and culture.

HARRY L. SHAPIRO, Chairman of the Department of Anthropology at the American Museum of Natural History, received his doctorate in physical anthropology from Harvard University in 1926. One of Dr. Shapiro's major interests in physical anthropology has been the study of race and race mixture.

H. M. WORMINGTON is Curator of Archaeology at the Denver Museum of Natural History, where she has worked since 1935. Dr. Wormington received her doctorate in anthropology from Harvard University in 1954. Her primary area of interest has been the archaeology of the American Southwest with a special emphasis upon the Paleo-Indian. Her publications include the important compilation of the data of this horizon, *Ancient Man in North America*.

Index of Persons and Works Cited

Index of Subjects

Academy of Natural Sciences, Philadelphia, 2, 13, 21, 135; Symposium on Early Man, 14, 56; skeletal material in, 14, 48-49, 60; Poinsett-Keating collection and, 40-42

Academy of Natural Sciences Museum, 135

Adaptation process, 52-53; cultural, 90, 110

Africa, 4, 63, 125

Agate Basin points, 57

Agriculture, 115

Ahwahharway Indians, 10n

Aivilik Eskimos, 97

Alabama, 59

Alarnerk, site, Canada, 85

Alaska, 58, 78, 79-100; Ipiutak theory and, 77, 82, 92; cultural traditions, hypotheses concerning, 89-90, 91-92, 93; language groups in, 94-96; ethnological study in, 96-100. *See also specific placenames*

Alaska, University of, 77, 89, 95

Albany, New York, 135

Aleutian Islands, 83, 92

Aleut-Konyag project, 81, 94

Aleuts, 78, 82-83, 87, 92, 97; linguistics and, 94-95

Algonkian Indians, 120-21; languages of, 36, 107, 119; kinship systems and, 109-10, 111, 112, 114-15, 116

American Academy of Arts and Sciences, Boston, 12n, 32

American Anthropological Association, *viii*, 2

American Antiquarian Society, 32

American Association for the Advancement of Science (AAAS), *viii*, 23, 25n

American Association of Physical Anthropologists, 16

American Folklore Society, *viii*

American Indian Ethnohistoric Conference, 118

"American Museum" of Du Simitière, 6n, 133

American Museum, of Peale, *vi*, 8

American Philosophical Society, 4, 12, 21, 32-46; Lewis and Clark expedition and, 6-7, 8, 15; Standing Committee on Antiquities, 6n, 35-36; Library, 32, 37n, 41, 42, 138; Historical and Literary Committee, 34, 36, 37; Philosophical Hall, 38, 40, 41, 42; *Classified Index*, 39; archaeological research grants, 57, 59-60, 61

American Revolution, 6, 10

Amherst College, 135

Anaktuvuk Pass, Alaska, 83

Anatomy, 14, 15, 47, 48-49, 50

Andes Mountains, 74

Andover, Massachusetts, 108

Angoon, Alaska, 85, 95, 97

Anthropological Society of London, 14

Anthropological Society of Paris, 14

Anthropological Society of Washington, 2-3, 24n

Anthropology: scientific status of, *vi-ix*, 10-11, 12, 13, 19, 22-27, 49, 50, 68, 137; American Philosophical Society and, 4, 12, 32-46, 59, 60, 61, 138; Arctic, 77-106; museum display techniques and, 140-42. *See also contributing disciplines*, i.e., Archaeology; Ethnology; Linguistics; Physical anthropology

Anthropometry, 11, 50